A Uniformed Response

Recollections of a Kent police officer from the 1960s

TONY KIRKBANK

authorHOUSE®

AuthorHouse™
1663 Liberty Drive
Bloomington, IN 47403
www.authorhouse.com
Phone: 1-800-839-8640

Published by AuthorHouse   09/11/2012

ISBN: 978-1-4678-8483-9 (sc)
ISBN: 978-1-4678-8484-6 (hc)
ISBN: 978-1-4678-8485-3 (e)

TABLE OF CONTENTS

PREFACE

IN 1962, I was sworn in as a constable in the Kent Police Force at a time when, generally, the public accepted and respected police officers for their duty and commitment, with that respect being returned. Police pay was poor. The hours were long and inconvenient. Personal equipment was minimal. There were no personal radios, no computers, no Crown Prosecution Service. The police officer was alone on his beat, took his own decisions as a self-disciplined individual and enjoyed his work.

This book covers the years between my recruitment and 1977, when I moved to the city of Canterbury. It details just some of the countless experiences encountered over the first fifteen of my thirty years' service in both the hot spots of urban policing in west Kent, to the more serene times spent as a rural policeman in east Kent. Many of the names have been changed.

Within the following text, I have sought to emphasise the attitude and work ethic that existed before 1984, a year when the national miners' strike and the Police & Criminal Evidence Act both took effect. These two events combined to totally change the way that police officers were regarded by the public and the media and how the police treated the public, leading to a widening of the gulf between them that may never be closed.

Whilst the heady days of policemen in dark blue uniforms patrolling in their pointed helmets are now in the past, I hope that these recollections of times gone by may be found both entertaining and thought-provoking to anyone who has a care for law and order in this country.

INTRODUCTION

My lasting recollection of Christmas 1962 was that of a truly white Christmas. Throughout southern England, and particularly in the county of Kent, the entire countryside lay under a thick carpet of snow which was to form the base for many subsequent falls that were to continue, almost unabated, for a further three months. This was to cause interruption and hardship for all of the people who struggled to maintain their usual way of life. Train services were severely disrupted, roads were regularly blocked by new snowfall and abandoned vehicles. Many people were unable to go about their normal day to day activities whilst temperatures remained stubbornly in the blue. It was in these numbing conditions that I was to commence pounding the beat and a thirty year commitment to public service. Was the public going to be ready for me?

Several months earlier, I had turned my back on a future in professional photography and went to my local police station at Margate for a job application form. Now as winter stretched its claws upon the downland and Weald of Kent, I had, modestly successfully, completed my initial three month training as a raw 19-year-old probationary police recruit.

A local induction course had been undertaken at the Kent Police Force HQ at Maidstone, where I had been taught about the measures and procedures and By-Laws that were to be complied with at my new posting.

At the end of this induction, about eight of us were bussed down to the Magistrates Court in Maidstone, where we were duly sworn in by the chief magistrate and told that we now each held the rank of Constable in the Kent County Constabulary with all the powers and responsibility attached to that ancient title.

Back at headquarters, it was rather disappointing to have been told by the training school sergeant that I was to be posted to a town called Dartford, which I had always thought was a part of London. I had grown up on the Kent coast, at Margate, where the sea air was fresh and bracing. I knew the area and had many friends and acquaintances that I was not happy to leave and had been hoping to get a local posting where I could keep my friends and make use of my local knowledge.

When the details were read out to us, and after speaking with my more geographically-aware colleagues, I realised that Dartford was the most distant posting within the county that it was possible to have.

So it was, on Thursday the 27th December 1962, that I arrived at Dartford railway station carrying my suitcase and wondering how to find the town's police station. The winter sun was making an effort to brighten the scene and I considered, rather inappropriately, that Dartford was quite an attractive town, covered as it was by a carpet of deep snow and with the pale yellow rays of the afternoon sun reflecting upon the lock-up shops along Station Approach. A change of mind was to overtake me when the thaw set in several weeks later.

There was little traffic on the streets as I dragged my belongings to Highfield Road where I entered the front door of Dartford "nick", to be welcomed by a friendly old station officer whom I got to know as Jack. Jack had a full head of silver hair and displayed a long row of colourful medal ribbons across his chest. I was to learn a lot from Jack in the weeks to come.

"Bring your bag in and go and make a brew," he said, directing me to the small kitchen at the end of the corridor behind the front office. "And you had better make a full pot, because the Chief will want one as well".

I opened the door from the public entrance hall and entered the working area of my first police station. It was warm and smelled of floor polish and stale cigarette smoke.

The woodwork was brown varnish, the floors were brown linoleum, the ancient table and chairs bore a dark brown patina that had obviously been built up over a great many years. The overflowing cabinets were brown, as were the lampshades, but that was because of the nicotine staining.

Apart from Jack, seated behind the main counter with his glasses perched on the end of his bulbous nose, the police station appeared to be deserted—and very brown.

"Where is everyone?" I asked.

"Who were you expecting?" he countered.

"I was told that Dartford was a busy town, so I expected to see more police officers here."

"It is a busy town, lad," said Jack. "That's why no-one's in 'ere."

Thus firmly put into my place, I followed Jack's directions to the kitchen and walked down the dark brown corridor and past an open office door where I saw the chief inspector sitting at his desk.

He looked up at me as I passed and said, "You the new bloke?" to which I replied that I was, and politely identified myself to him.

"Two sugars then, lad." He said informally, and went back to his book. I continued down the corridor where I found a small kitchen area with the essentials for a work environment—a kettle and a tea caddy. I immediately felt that a life of being a copper would be OK after all.

Dartford Police Station
© Kent Police Museum

CHAPTER 1

The Kent Police Force

THE KENT COUNTY Constabulary was formed in 1857 under their first Chief Constable, John Ruxton, with headquarters at Wrens Cross in Maidstone town centre. In the 19th century, policing was more territorial with county forces operating side by side with the old borough forces within the county. Boroughs such as Margate, Ramsgate, Tunbridge Wells and some other large towns, operated their own local police under the control of local Watch Committees. Under normal circumstances, county officers did not normally encroach into the specified boroughs and *vice versa*. However, powers had been granted to all police officers that allowed them to operate legally and officially within any adjoining county or borough. It was not until the 1950s that the Borough forces were integrated into the wider county police force and the Police Acts gave national powers within England and Wales for legal authority. The atmosphere of policing was very parochial with great respect being given and received between police and public.

In these modern times, it is now known as the Kent Police Service, possibly to reflect the political intention of exhibiting a more caring nature of policing within the United Kingdom, albeit that a normal dark blue police tunic and traditional helmet has been replaced with high-visibility jackets, anti-stab vests, CS gas containers, firearms-equipped officers and other modes of self-protection and aggression. That image does not elicit respect from anyone, honest or otherwise.

In those heady days of 1962 the constabulary had their main headquarters building in Sutton Road, in the county town of Maidstone. This site had been purchased in 1934 after the previous, original headquarters at Wrens Cross in the town centre had been deemed too small.

An imposing purpose-built building, set back in its own grounds, it consisted of a main block containing all of the administrational offices, an operations room (known as Ops) and related specialist areas. Connected to this main block were matching east wing and west wing extensions.

The east wing housed primarily the No.1 Area Traffic Garage and HQ Stores whilst the west wing contained the kitchen/ restaurant areas, with accommodation rooms on the upper floor for residential courses, training and CID.

Now, well into the 21st Century, the original building still keeps its facade but the accumulation of many new additions to the rear, and over much of the original green site, has created an administrative built-up area that incorporates a new Communications Centre, Training Centre and ancillary areas connected with a busy police organisation.

The number of actual police officers serving in Kent has probably doubled in 50 years from nearly 2,000 in 1965 to 3,800 in 2009, but the number of civilian employees now connected with the administration and legal aspects of police work must have increased ten-fold or more.

As most police work is regarded as "Immediate"—meaning that police deal with an incident, normally without too much delay, and then leave to do the paperwork—one wonders whether such a top-heavy civilian presence is really necessary in the pursuit of modern policing.

I initially attended our Force HQ during the summer of 1962; first for my entrance exam, then, having been successful in that examination, for my formal interview with the recruitment officer. I considered that I was fortunate to be accepted as a probationer constable as I had previously attempted to join the Police Cadet Force but failed to get accepted, probably because I still suffered from a childhood speech problem that caused me to stammer. I managed to overcome nervousness and was told that I was to become a police officer at the age of 19 years and one week.

I hurried home to Margate where I proposed to my then girlfriend, who accepted, and we commenced a two-year engagement period.

I spent a further day in Maidstone getting measured up and fitted with my first uniform at the H.Q. Stores department. The allocation included two winter-weight tunics, three pairs of winter weight trousers, a heavy raincoat, three blue shirts (no collars attached), ten collars—starched, two helmets, two pairs of black leather gloves and one pair of white ceremonial gloves, a pocket book holder, a chrome whistle on a chain to be worn through the top button of the tunic, a metal torch, a pair of Hiatt handbolts as featured in Victorian times and, best of all, a used lignite truncheon which still bore signs of action from its murky past.

We were expected to obtain our own boots, for which we received an allowance in our pay of a few pence a week. Thus fully equipped for the rigours of police work, I was now ready to be trained.

CHAPTER 2

Training

BACK IN THE 1960s, all new probationer constables spent the first 13 weeks out of reach of the general public, which was probably a good thing for both the public, and us. My initial police training started in September 1962, and was carried out at the No. 6 District Police Training Centre, which was located in the old Star & Garter Home overlooking the town of Sandgate, near Folkestone, with panoramic views across the English Channel and Romney Marsh. The Training School had originally opened at this location in Easter 1946.

The term, No 6 District referred to the area covered by the training centre, and included the counties of Kent, Surrey, West Sussex, East Sussex and Hampshire. The City force of Southampton and the Channel Isles (Jersey and Guernsey) also made up the mix, leading to friendships and contacts amongst the recruits that would last many years.

This shared training system had been operating country-wide for many years as it mattered not where you came from in England or Wales—the law was standard. Local by-laws were taught later at local level. It was a system that worked and allowed for a steady stream of trained officers to perform to a necessary standard. North of the border, in Scotland, a slightly different legal system is in operation and the police forces there act under the control of the police authority, the chief constable and the Secretary of State for Scotland. Their court procedure also differs from that used in England and Wales.

England and Wales police training was later re-organised at county level, with No 6 District becoming defunct. Indeed, one of the new buildings at Sutton Road, Maidstone, now houses the Kent Police Training School, with other neighbouring counties also having their own facilities. Of recent years, it has become popular to consider more centralisation, especially of police forces, so expect training to revert to the District model very soon. *Plus ça change.*

The main building of the training centre at Sandgate, or Enbrook House as it was once known, was originally a large stately 19th century house with an imposing porte cochere, or covered entry, designed for the Victorian "coach and four" to discharge its passengers to the front door in comfort. Enbrook House had originally been constructed in the 1850s in the gothic style. After being purchased as a "Star & Garter Home" for wounded servicemen from the First World War in 1920, only the original East Wing remained, and the main three-storey building was constructed in the Cape Colonial style between 1924 and 1928. What grandeur to endure for the next thirteen weeks.

The building stood in its extensive grounds with the main frontage facing south across the English Channel. The walls were whitewashed which gave it a Mediterranean appearance. To the front of the main building was a large paved area with seating. Beyond that pleasant patio were the lawned gardens bordered by mature trees. Additional single-storey buildings had been added at the rear of the main house in recent years to provide classrooms.

In the 1970s, the Home Office, in one of their regular modernisation programmes, saw fit to close the training centre as part of a re-organisation and sold the building and grounds to a large travel company for use as their UK headquarters.

Subsequent improvements led to the demolishing of this beautiful classic building and the erection of a steel and concrete edifice which would never compare to the architecture of the old.

On entering the main entrance through the grand porte cochere, a dark oak panelled reception area gave a subdued welcome to the newcomer. Whilst in the main body of the building, large windows provided a bright interior with high ceilings and views to the south across Sandgate. Beyond the reception area were the administrational areas and social rooms, including a large dining room and kitchen. Upstairs were the dormitories where the manly skills of boxing beds and polishing toecaps until they reflected like mirrors were to be learned.

The new recruits to this training centre all came from the home counties of England and were from all walks of life. Some were ex-forces and already well-disciplined in their behaviour, albeit a different type of discipline to that needed to be a constable in those days.

The obedience enforced upon forces personnel was a group discipline whereby a private soldier was answerable to his corporal, and he, in turn, to the sergeant. Squads carried out group duties and instead of making their own individual decisions, were responsible as a squad for carrying out current orders.

Police discipline was far more individual with the constable expected to assess a situation or occurrence on his own and take the appropriate action to resolve that matter himself, to the later satisfaction of his superior officers who might be armed with a Policy Book. This is called self-discipline and was a necessary skill of any individual police officer.

Other recruits were from various employments or professions who just wanted a change of direction in the way they earned their money.

The last classification of recruits were the young ex-police cadets who generally considered themselves to already be good policemen because they had been wearing a navy-blue uniform in public and had been out walking the beat, even though it had been whilst accompanied by a regular officer and they had been told that they couldn't touch anything.

I had fallen into the second category. After leaving school at 15 years of age, I had taken up a career as a photographic apprentice with a local photographer and photographic dealer situated in Marine Gardens at Margate.

The workings of the camera were taught to me, together with the techniques of studio and wedding photography, retail photography and sales, as well as skills in the darkroom, developing and printing photographic items.

I gained experience of medical photography and became used to the sight of gory wounds through attending at the local hospital and helping to take progress photographs of the treatment of some gruesome injuries that had been caused to members of the public in all sorts of accidents.

After three years of such toil and experience, I was to find out later on in my service that this background would be of absolutely no use whatsoever to me in the next thirty years.

No. That's not exactly right. My extensive experience of finding my way around in the total darkness of the film development room did help me on occasions during night duty when the torch battery went flat.

All of us at Sandgate were male entrants because, in those distant days, women were recruited in considerably lower numbers than their male counterparts and they received additional specialist training at all-female training centres. Their teaching was, like ours, in all the main facets of traffic and criminal law, with rather more attention to the more caring disciplines, such as child law and other matters which pertained to their gender.

The male entrants were taught the strict and often painful disciplines of police behaviour by the Law & Procedure instructors,

Physical Training instructor (PTI) and the Drill instructor, albeit in their different ways. Humour was rarely encountered, other than during lectures on sexual offences which frequently brought out the baser characteristics of the participants in an all male classroom.

The PTI, Sergeant Walters, was an upright, stern-looking man who always seemed to wear the same track suit bottoms and a sleeveless vest which showed off his upper body muscles and threatening tattoos in a rather macho way, especially compared to beanpole types such as myself.

During my teenage years, I had never gone in for the type of activities that build muscle and stamina. My post-school exercise had been limited to three years of work in a photographic film processing environment where any sudden movement could cause bruising from unseen equipment! This darkened work environment also accounted for my pale and spotty complexion.

On our first day of proper training at Sandgate there were two periods of what turned out to be rather harsh physical exercise where the staff obviously wanted to assess the fitness, or otherwise, of these pathetic young men. Accordingly, "Punchy" Walters had our entire course intake lined up on the immaculate lawns in front of the main building and we were told to do as many press-ups as we could. I think I managed as many as eight before collapsing in a heap, only to be cajoled and threatened to continue well past the point of exhaustion.

One lad was physically sick but that made no difference to Punchy's screaming and ranting.

This activity was followed by other gymnastic atrocities and concluded with several circuits of the grounds, known loosely as "some gentle cross-country", accompanied by a screaming instructor seemingly hell-bent on causing as much discomfort as he could manage.

Why, for Heaven's sake, had I left the passive enjoyment of photographic work to undergo this attack upon the extremes of my bodily capabilities?

There was little doubt that my own stamina was somewhat below the average displayed by our intake. It was expected, then, that when his instructional periods involved subjects like physical interaction, or unarmed combat, Punchy Walters used to pick on me so that he could demonstrate his undoubted skills as a self-defence expert, bully and oppressor.

Self-defence training is all very well, but, being on the receiving end most of the time, you don't actually get to practice using the skills that the instructor wished to impart to the rest of the laughing gallery.

Around this time, a TV presenter, Kent Walton, was a commentator on a programme shown every Saturday afternoon loosely referred to as Professional Wrestling. In these bouts, the opponents would assault and wrestle each other to submission but rarely were there any serious injuries. I understand that all the professional wrestlers were members of the Actors' Union. After years of watching this thrilling and seemingly violent entertainment, viewers were experts in the wrestling holds and throws, with all the moves appearing simple and uncomplicated. The more so after a session of alcohol!

Unlike the actors in the ring, who have their own, and their opponents' welfare to consider, drunken people just don't fight fair! Young men have always emulated the professional fighter, especially after leaving the pub or club late at night having imbibed to excess upon the various liquids provided for their hard-earned pounds. The consequence is frequently for the need of the police to be able to match, or curtail the violence, nearly always with controlled violence of their own.

This is, therefore, the reason for us to be trained in the art of self-defence and controlled ability to overcome the miscreant who wants to fight everyone. That is all very well, but I was always the one who seemed to get bruised.

It all came good for me one day. A new intake of recruits was being entertained by Punchy in his own inimitable way. He selected one of their members to come forward and he said to the puny young man in the baggy shorts, "Come at me as if you had a knife." The young man did as he was told and went through the motions of lunging forward with the right hand extended, as if holding a weapon.

Punchy grabbed his arm and twisted it as if to lock out the elbow at a painful angle against the joint, in the approved method of any bully PTI, to inflict agony. Within a split second there was a whirling of bodies and associated screams which ending up with Punchy Walters lying on his back in front of the ex-corporal of the Parachute Regiment, nursing a broken arm. "Sorry" said the ex-para, "but you almost hurt me." An early lesson learned for me, that the small ones can often be the most dangerous.

Punchy was also in charge of us on the few occasions when we were all bussed to the grand-sounding Folkestone Municipal Swimming Baths—long since demolished—which had been built many years earlier at the base of the Leas Cliff towards the west side of the town. The bus in which were transported was also a cause for anxious recollection. It was probably a post-war Foden charabanc equipped with a very worn-out diesel engine which emitted vast clouds of smoke and fumes. The gearbox had precious few cogs left on the wheels, those that were still present made continuous crunching and grinding sounds. The clutch slipped when going uphill and the seating was always musty, damp and uncomfortable.

Later in my life, when I rose to the heights of a "traffic cop", I would be removing such death traps from the road.

On reaching the swimming pool, there were never any other patrons present. This might have been regarded as unusual, apart from the fact that by 1962 the Folkestone Municipal Pool was deemed by the local council to be condemned and therefore permanently closed to the public. I believe that the Police Training Centre held one of the only two keys to the huge rusty padlock on the gate.

The facilities were baser than a plain brick-wall toilet and, accordingly, the water was an unusual shade of green with extraordinary floating things on the surface. A net on the end of a long bamboo cane facilitated the removal of the strangest bits prior to our timid entry into the gloomy water. Above the murky waters, there was a roof made of iron and concrete beams. The amount of glass remaining in place was somewhat less than the architect had planned for and this allowed the gull and starling population of the East Kent coastal region to share the delights of this amenity.

It was in this vile soup that we were taught how to save people from drowning—and from toxic poisoning as well, I expect. It was difficult to argue the case for better conditions for training when Punchy explained that you cannot always choose the best conditions to save somebody in real life.

Thus, I became fully qualified to be a lifesaver with an addendum to the certificate quoting special skills in cesspit evacuation.

Sergeant Will Sellars was the Drill Sergeant. He was a Gentleman of the County of Kent and a smarter individual you would rarely meet. His previous military service as a NCO showed, as he was always immaculately turned out with boots and buttons that shone like mirrors, knife-edge creases down his trousers and a brightly polished slashed peak to his flat hat. He sported a polished mahogany swagger stick with a shiny silver knob which was a natural extension of his right arm and it was one of his duties to ensure that we were similarly smartly attired with bulled boots and razor-sharp creases to our trousers and uniform sleeves.

Daily inspections carried out by him on the parade ground were highly critical of the hirsute appearance of some recruits, leading to regular work for the visiting hairdresser who, no doubt, probably retired to some tropical paradise on the profits of his profession.

My own length of hair was immediately the subject of adverse comment from the drill sergeant, resulting in my having to visit the hairdresser that same week. The problem was that I had no spare cash. I was able to coerce another recruit to wager me the costs of the hair-cut if I had a head shave. The result satisfied the drill sergeant and I suffered a head cold for weeks.

In accordance with Sergeant Sellars tasks in making us into a smart body of Police Officers, an inordinate amount of time was spent on demonstrating the correct way to wear the police helmet with almost religious zeal applied to the distance of a single thumb-joint to be the guide as to the space between the tip of the nose and the front peak of the police helmet. The chin strap could only pass over the point of the chin and the nap of the material from which the helmet was made was to be visibly smoothed downwards by continuous brushing. I had thought that putting on a hat was easy.

Most mornings started with a period of drill, which comprised of twenty minutes of marching and counter marching across the parade ground until the soles of our feet stung. Next, we were instructed in the art of manual traffic control. We were taught the correct deportment to provide clear, unambiguous arm signals from the front, from either side and from behind until our arms were dropping with muscle fatigue.

This was, at last, followed by the instruction "Time for a little whoa!" At which command we would adjourn to the old greenhouse, where, in a gentle relaxed manner, out of sight of the prying eyes of senior officers, we were permitted to smoke a cigarette or two and appreciate the humanity of the man.

I don't know how he did it but, in twelve weeks of intermittent drill practice, he honed us from a collection of ill-disciplined rabble into a smart squad of well turned-out uniformed officers. We marched smartly around the parade ground, carrying out reverse manoeuvres, right and left wheels, and ordered saluting to the front and to the side with almost Grenadier Guards precision. Well, I thought so at the time. All of us seemed to manage, and even enjoy, drill.

Except, that is, for poor Pc Fry who never did get the hang of swinging the left arm/right leg, right arm/left leg. Strange how a very intelligent individual with otherwise excellent fluidity of movement would only march left arm/left leg but there is, I am informed, always one man in any such unit who cannot co-ordinate his body movements.

On passing-out day, we arranged for him to be hidden in the middle of the squad.

Pc Fry did have one great gift that everyone within a mile or so was to realise. On individual inspection by a senior officer, we were required to identify ourselves, and our county or city force, at the top of our voice. I'm sure that the inspecting officer, be it Sergeant Sellars or the Commandant, always took a step backwards when facing this young man as his "Pc Fry. Southampton. Sir!" was expressed at something in excess of 125 decibels.

Our particular class of twelve was fortunate to have Sergeant Mallard as the class instructor. Again, like the other instructors, he was long in service and patience. His earlier policing days had been spent policing the mean streets of Weybridge as a Surrey Constabulary officer where he had acquired several years of practical experience. This experience, together with his knowledge of law and procedure, made him a highly effective instructor.

All subjects were covered within the stipulated periods so that we could assimilate the intricacies of Statute Law and Common Law, which in turn was sub-divided into larceny, burglary, buggery, piracy, Road Traffic Law and the rest of it. Then it was on to gambling, licensing, children in circuses and strange Latin terms, such as *mens rea*. What was all that about? Would I be qualified as a lawyer after all this?

Later in the course, we were instructed on the Diseases of Animals Act and like legislation. Ask any old copper what epizootic lymphangitis is and he will knowledgeably inform you that it is a

Part 1 notifiable disease to be found in sheep. Perhaps we could also qualify as veterinary surgeons as well?

There was little time for freedom to relax. The regime was based upon a mixture of National Service training and a US Army Boot Camp. After morning reveille, beds in the dormitories had to be stripped off and cleared. Formal boxing of the bed then took place. This meant a precise folding of each sheet and blanket.

These items were then placed, sandwich-fashion, at the head of the bed with one remaining blanket wrapped around the whole to make a tidy, square box of bedding. Some of the ex-forces recruits showed us how to use sheets of cardboard to stiffen the sides and maintain the required square shape of the box but surely this was going too far. The pillows were smoothed and placed on top in immaculate order.

Each individual was responsible for his own bed-space, or "pit" as it was known, and it became a matter of pride not to let the standard fall. This tidy bed was also the base layout for kit inspection when ordered. In this event, additionally, the personal contents of the officer's kit cabinet were displayed upon the bed in a regimented and pre-ordained way. Why? This is called discipline and must not be questioned at all.

Every few days the inspection was undertaken by a more senior officer who was probably seconded to the training centre because of his skill in the identification of rogue specks of dust on distant skirting board ledges within the dormitory. His subsequent discovery of any dust or fluff that had not been removed by the dormitory occupants invariably led to additional periods of dusting and polishing to a level worthy of the cleanest space satellite laboratory.

Having been passed as acceptable (no-one received higher praise than this) by the duty instructor, we had our breakfast in the mess room, followed by revision of past lecture sessions, and of Definitions.

Definitions were contained in a small yellow booklet and were a source of learning, parrot-fashion, short phrases and sentences which were to remain fixed in our brains forever. E.g. *"Definition 1. A Constable is a citizen, locally appointed but having authority under the Crown for the protection of life and property, maintenance of public order, the prevention and detection of crime and the prosecution of offenders against the peace."* Even after over 50 years, the words flood so easily back.

Please note that the words, "prosecution of offenders" comes fourth in the list . . .

Other entries in the book defined the essential ingredients necessary to prove offences, such as larceny, arson, rape, road traffic law and so forth. There were over 150 of them to be committed to memory with daily tests carried out by the instructors.

The advantage to police officers in those days was that Statute Laws had stood for a great many years without having undergone major changes. The Larceny Act 1861, the Offences Against the People Act 1861 and Town Police Clauses Act 1847 were among the many major Statutes that were still valid and these gave clear, unambiguous wording to specify offences, provided police powers and defined penalties.

Two years earlier, the government had enacted the Road Traffic Act 1960 which was a major piece of legislation, now embedded in our learning, which stood for 28 years and replaced the old act of 1933.

Case Law had clarified specific points within the Statutes but the basic rules withstood time. Compare that with the new Regulations and Instruments created in all areas of law by parliament that allow the legal profession to become profligate in their pursuit of greater profit from the perceived law-breaker.

Surely, it is poor practice to keep making even more specific statute laws when the number of police officers available on the streets to enforce them is dwindling.

Consider the present laws to prohibit the use of mobile phones whilst driving. There was a perfectly good section under the Construction and Use Regulations which states that it is an offence to drive a motor vehicle on a road whilst not being in proper control. Many police officers, including myself, have reported drivers under this section for such things as reading a book, opening a packet of sweets, drinking from a bottle and other actions which would cause the mind to wander from driving skill.

To then make a specific law regarding mobile phones and not to include similar items such as Dictaphones, or even CB-type two-way radios, defies belief that the law-makers could be so naïve. The magistrates are in the best position to assess the gravity of each offence and act accordingly under the existing legislation.

Law was much more black and white in 1962!

I am sure that much of the current desire to update our statutes is the fault of the legal profession seeking any little wording and twisting it around to save their clients from commonsense prosecution.

Take the offence of driving a car whilst intoxicated. The law stated that a "Police Officer in uniform" can stop such a motorist and demand that a suspected inebriated driver take a breath test. Such simple words but they failed to qualify what a "uniform" was! A case went all the way through our legal system to the highest court in the land, where it was decided that, if the police officer was not wearing his hat, he was not in uniform. Even though he was wearing a police tunic, driving a police car and using police apparatus to carry out the test, he was deemed to be not in uniform as laid down in the Act.

What next? He wasn't displaying his whistle chain?

A loophole had been found and the drunken driver got off the charge totally free. Similarly, well-known solicitors specialise in representing well-heeled individuals and seek obscure let-outs that lead to acquittal—even though commonsense demands that the guilt is complete.

Out of the classroom at 5 o'clock, and at the end of the students' normal working day, there were further extended revision periods wherever one could find a quiet seat. There was also uniform to be pressed, boot bulling to be undertaken and collar washing to be done.

Back then, each officer was issued with three detachable collars to each shirt. The thought of a daily change of shirt was unheard of.

The recruits who had served in the armed forces were lauded as excellent tutors in the black art of spit & polish. It is a method of shining leather that is not as easy and quick as you think. Only one small cloth and a tin of Cherry Blossom blacking were required for the process.

The method was to lift a lump of blacking from the tin and rub it over the surface of the toecap in a circular motion for as long as it took to become a mirror-like surface. The addition of frequent globs of spittle aided the process which took a minimum of thirty minutes per toecap.

Insomniacs took the process several stages further so that the entire boot became like lustrous patent leather. Additionally, the use of a heated spoon handle removed the pimples in the leather of the cheaper "Doc Martins" boots so as to provide a smooth surface for shining.

Now we knew what the ex-forces entrants did when they were not on the drill square or peeling potatoes.

Most police recruits had two pairs of boots for daily use; the bulled pair for wearing during parade and drill, so as not to upset Sergeant Sellars, and a normal, albeit very shiny pair, for use around the classrooms.

To get us ready for patrolling the mean streets, recruits were detailed to carry out frequent tasks as security patrols around the grounds.

Duty rotas were drawn up by the Instructors Office and duty students were nominated to wear their uniforms beyond the usual class periods. They were then given a torch and instructed to patrol the grounds and out-buildings until a late hour (after the bar had closed!). A log sheet had to be maintained and it was not unknown for an instructor to deliberately unlock some distant, rarely-used entrance, just to see if the student was conscientious in his evening checks.

There were few opportunities to make any trips into the nearby town, which was, perhaps, best because police pay at the time was abysmal. Besides that, Folkestone town centre during late autumn into winter was a dreadful place to seek entertainment.

Because Folkestone was a garrison town, with Shornecliffe Barracks only a mile away, there was always likely to be some interaction between rival groups of young males seeking to prove their mettle.

We used to have what was known as "Pay Parade" each month, where we all lined up in the main corridor and then had to step forward to the pay table to receive our monthly money in banknote and coin, followed by a smart salute to the paymaster. It was only after I had been at my first posting for a year or so that the payment of salaries by cash on parade was ceased and the issue of pay cheques was commenced.

So passed thirteen weeks of PT, drill, law and procedure, staged incidents and all the other facets of training that were designed to bring the raw young man up to the required standard before launching him upon an unsuspecting public. The autumn colours faded and the leaves fell around the wooded grounds of the lovely building at which we were receiving our training.

There was a television and music centre for those who had already completed their day's tasks, or of patrolling the grounds of the training centre, learning definitions and other course work. Problems encountered with this modern technology included the fact that the television aerial was little more than a length of lighting flex nailed to the wall resulting in an unwatchable picture, and the music centre had a defective tuner. The record player part of the music centre did work, but with only a Frank Sinatra LP and a much scratched Paul Anka rendering of "Oh, Please, Diana" to listen to, most lads went back to the book of Definitions.

It was one event that autumn that actually stopped the lessons whilst we all listened to the news. President Kennedy had threatened Khrushchev over the "Weapons to Cuba" incident.

All of us, even those normally oblivious to life outside our closed community, gathered around a small transistor radio outside the classroom on 28th October waiting for the four-minute warning to be announced.

There was genuine relief expressed when the news came through that we were not to be involved in any nuclear conflict. Such threats were taken extremely seriously in those days and we were all very well briefed on the consequences of such a conflict affecting us in Britain.

The thought of ordinary police officers being armed and shooting looters in the streets was not what we had joined for, but the possibility of such actions were made abundantly clear to us during that area of training.

It was around this time that the film, *A War Game*, was made in and around the Medway Towns in Kent. It was probably the most harrowing film ever made which depicted a nuclear attack on an urban area.

It was, in fact, so harrowing that it was banned from UK public screening until 1985, but I do recall that it was shown to police officers as an information film on what would occur if we were drawn into such a terrible conflict with our enemies.

Armed Kent police shooting at looters in Chatham was, at the time, fictional, but honestly based on what could have truly happened had the bomb dropped. It was this scenario that was to have a strong background feature in our training in the follow years.

Course 189 finished a few days before Christmas 1962 and the class photographs were duly taken. Postings were allocated and the end of course party was endured through a shared alcoholic haze. The course instructors became friends and were now regarded as fellow human beings.

We had appreciated their efforts after all, regardless of the initial (and often, continued) badgering in the knowledge that they had been there and done it.

I recall Sergeant Mallard passing on his final words of wisdom to us. He told us that we could be called to every sort of incident we could ever think of; to cats up trees, to domestic disputes, to road traffic accidents, to major disasters.

As you make the first uniformed approach to the incident, a member of the public would recognise you and say, "Ah! Here comes a policeman!" You would now be expected to take charge of the scenario with total expertise and confidence, seeing it through by correct and judicious decision-making to the satisfaction of both the public and your superior officers when they studied your report.

Now it was going to be our turn to experience the feeling that you really didn't know what was going to happen next—but you would have to deal with it anyway. It would be an example of self-discipline, experience and knowledge being applied to the art of policing.

Just a few more days of a local induction course at Maidstone Headquarters and I would be set free amongst the good, and bad, citizens of Dartford.

Chapter 3

Welcome to Dartford Nick

For a single policeman, the first essential when posted to a town away from home, was to find a place to stay, preferably not too dissimilar to what he was used to in Civvy Street. This usually meant a move into lodgings. In the front office, most police stations had an exercise book underneath the counter which listed the "digs" available to single officers in the town and in easy reach of the police station. Landladies, or any other lonely old spinster or widow who needed a young man as live-in company, would leave their details with the station officer, stating that they had a room available to young police officers. The main advantages of this type of accommodation were that meals were usually available when they were needed, albeit at odd times of the day, washing of clothes, both personal and uniform articles, was done for you, your bed was usually made and there was little tidying up to do. In other words, from someone who was spoilt by their mother, with the right landlady, it was just like home!

In more modern times, the landlady as we knew her has disappeared and young men find apartments where the takeaway pizza rules supreme, together with the unspeakable mess that accumulates from lack of housekeeping.

It was one of the tasks of the duty inspector to do what his name implied, and "inspect" the lodgings to see if they were suitable as full board accommodation for young men living away from the parental home for the first time. The arrangements were duly checked and passed, following which, new single officers would be allocated those digs for the duration of their posting, or until they found an alternative (or a wife, perhaps!).

From my own experience at Dartford, I am sure that part of the criteria for becoming a probationer policeman's landlady was that she should be an elderly widow with a beard.

Senior officers did not seem to have a lot of faith in the off-duty behaviour of their young constables and tended not to allow these vulnerable young men to have any chance of being tempted by the attractions of some female landlady who exhibited possible charms or talents that might, even remotely, lead to sexual attraction.

One of the fully established constables based at Dartford was Spud Taylor. He was a very extrovert young man and if he had had a family motto, it would probably have been "*petere illecebra ubi nullus*" or, roughly translated, "Seek temptation when there is none".

Spud had initially been lodged with a kindly old lady in Chastillian Road but the location and atmosphere was far too quiet and the list of the landlady's restrictions on his life there became too much for him. Consequently, he sought out new digs and found an attractive middle-aged lady whose husband was known to be a merchant seaman. She had a spare room available on a full board arrangement and he eagerly moved in. It took very little time for his natural instincts to take over and, less than a week later, within ten minutes of the husband's unexpected return from Tilbury Docks at one o'clock in the morning, Spud's colleagues were called to the first domestic violence call at the new digs.

Not to be deterred, Spud then moved in with a widow in her 30s, having had cause to deal with a domestic incident which led to the chance meeting with her, and they were later married, but not for long. His relationships were always a good excuse to indulge in idle gossip.

My digs were already settled for me before I arrived. I was to be lodged with dear old Mrs Whitehead. She was the elderly owner of a large semi-detached house fronting the main A2 arterial route into London, known as Princes Road.

An inspector from Dartford Police Station took me through the deepening snow out to these new lodgings on the outskirts of town. Before he slithered off back to the police station in the battered old Hillman Minx, he gave me a duty roster which showed that I was to be on Two Section and was to report for duty at 10pm the following day. Nights? So soon? He told me that I could go in during the day to find my way around, but I would still have to be back on duty at 10pm because they were short of manpower.

Mrs Whitehead was a lovely lady. She had been widowed during the war and enjoyed having lodgers. She had previously taken in teachers and I was to be her first policeman. Something about the "security of having a uniformed man about" she said. Not much good if I am always on nights, I told her.

Within a few weeks, I realised that I was, indeed, a very fortunate young man to have landed with such a great landlady. She even used to get up at 4.30am to cook my breakfast before I trudged off to the police station for a 5.45am start, complete with a breakfast box—which contained the ingredients for yet another breakfast at my morning break!

Her home was one of those houses that were stuck in a time warp. It was immaculately clean but had last been decorated by her husband before he left home to tackle the Hun some 20 years earlier. There actually was an aspidistra on the table in the front room and a smell of carbolic pervaded the house. All meals were taken in the kitchen, other than on Sunday, when the dining room was utilised. We didn't use the front room. That was for special guests and something called laying out. It was a few months before I knew what that meant.

As a naive 19 year old male, I quickly learnt that offering to do the odd things around the house led to benefits. Being the son of a builder and decorator, I was not entirely useless in the art of do-it-yourself and associated practical work. Minor and, later, some major decorating was undertaken, windows were cleaned, washers were changed and electrical devices were updated and fixed.

Such efforts ensured a very happy relationship between lodger and landlady, which saved much money on eating out and taking the clothes home for my mother to wash!

Getting to and from duty was a problem for me whilst I lived at Mrs Whitehead's home. It was about 2 miles distant from the town centre and, for the first three months of living there, everything was snowed up.

Not having access to any alternative means of transport, I was obliged to walk between home and the police station across snow-covered fields and blocked roads; a journey that took nearly an hour.

It was the end of March before ever I realised that there was a lay-by outside the house, so bad had been the wintry conditions.

Frequent heavy snowfall and Arctic temperatures throughout January and February made conditions continually difficult and when it wasn't snowing, the temperatures plunged to numbingly low numbers.

At nearby Stone, several lorries had, one awful day, made efforts to leave the A2 in a heavy blizzard, seeking an alternative route around abandoned cars that blocked the carriageway in both directions, and were themselves stuck in snow drifts which built up to 10 feet high. And there they remained, trapped, for several weeks before the snow ploughs could reach them. The drivers had been forced to leave the trucks and find accommodation in nearby villages, which made the situation worse because the snow ploughs could not work around them.

One February night, during my first stint of 14 nights straight off, I was on 3 beat, which bounded the Metropolitan area of Crayford on the west side of town. It was three o'clock in the morning and I was making a "point" on Crayford Road. (A "point" was a static pre-arranged position, usually by a telephone box, where the patrolling officer is expected to remain for fifteen minutes in case the sergeant requires him for a task—long before the days of personal radios, etc.)

Adjacent to me was a chemist shop with one of the old metal plate thermometers on the wall. The markings were in Fahrenheit and the number scale went down to 0 degrees. I could just see the top level of the mercury at 0 degrees, immediately above the bulb. 32 degrees Fahrenheit of frost (or -17C if that is better understood)!

Whilst contemplating the fact that I should have put another copy of the Daily Express between my vest and my pyjamas, underneath my thick serge uniform and greatcoat, I saw a car coming up the hill towards me. It was a blue Austin A60 van with a blue light on top—the night duty sergeant was driving towards me.

Sergeant Wills was a kindly man. Close to his retirement, he was regarded as a good common sense copper who was able to dispense sensible advice and guidance without being officious or haughty. The van pulled up in the hard frozen slush and the passenger window was lowered an inch. "Jump in, lad." he said. I needed no second instruction. I jumped into the passenger seat and slammed the door so as to keep the warm air enclosed within the tin box. This was to be my first ride in a marked police car—or so I thought. "All correct, Sarge." I said to him, in what I expected to be the accepted terminology. He then turned off the engine and we sat there in silence for about three minutes, when he said to me, "I'll sign your pocketbook for 3:05am. You can carry on now and I'll see you back at the nick at five-to-six—so you will have a few minutes to warm up before you go home."

That was it! Back into the freezing starlit night for another three hours, yet his generosity in allowing this poor wretched probationer to sit in his car for three minutes was, in my eyes, boundless. It was also apparent that riding round the town in police cars was not for the probationer constable. For one thing, there were very few police cars to ride around in.

When the big thaw came, we spent a lot of time helping householders whose pipes had burst, as well as other incidents caused by the extremes of the winter's weather.

My own lodgings, as at most properties in that row of houses, had also completely frozen up, with the consequential burst pipes causing quite severe problems for Mrs Whitehead. At least I was able to provide her with the necessary help in making the rooms habitable again.

One night, a major robbery/assault investigation was started when an elderly, well-dressed man had been found, well after midnight, unconscious in the ice and slush of the High Street with serious head wounds. Before police got there, he had been taken to hospital by ambulance.

The ambulance crew had reported that he appeared to have been attacked around his head and rendered severely injured. A search was made by night duty officers and the cause of his trauma was soon realised when a huge block of ice suddenly fell from an adjacent roof, narrowly causing similar problems for the night-duty CID officer who was almost directly underneath the ice slide. Some icicles that winter were several feet long and many were so huge that their weight pulled down sections of guttering as well as pipes and tiles.

The man duly recovered and he later confirmed that he had indeed been deluged by a shower of ice from a shop roof.

Within a few weeks' experience of Police Station life, it became clear that I was going to learn a lot in this interesting town. The police officers attached to the station were few in number but willing in spirit, and were always keen to give assistance and advice. Because the work-load was high, the adherence to a rigid procedure was often rather relaxed.

A strong sense of humour, frequently rather black, was evident with nearly everyone happy to share tasks even though their own work folders were loaded.

This high work load was, I found, a very regional experience within the Kent policing area. I had realised that Dartford was, indeed, a very busy town for all types of police work but it was only after a return home to Margate one weekend in March that I was to discover the wide disparity between East and West Kent.

I was walking to my parents' home late one evening and met a patrolling officer in the main street of Margate. He recognised me first. After all, everyone in uniform looks similar in the dark. Gordon had been on Course 189 with me at Sandgate a few months earlier and it was interesting to chat with him and compare notes.

He had actually been brought up in the neighbouring town of Ramsgate so had a good local knowledge of his area of policing and, indeed, was still living with his mother at the family home. He agreed that he had been very fortunate to be given a local posting but thought things were "a bit slow".

On exchanging details of our respective workloads, he indicated to me that he had already attended an accident and reported some people for minor parking and lighting regulations. "Yes", I said, "What else?" He gave me a blank look and said, "Not much else, really. The senior blokes get all the work, don't they?"

He was astonished when I told him that I had already been assaulted a couple of times; had arrested several people for crime and drunkenness offences; had both attended and reported several serious road traffic accidents and that my "in" tray was overflowing with outstanding paperwork. I couldn't tell if he was envious or relieved that he had experienced such a quiet three months in the job.

Gordon spent all his service in the Margate area, retiring as a sergeant, but during the times that we met socially over the years, he never gave me cause to believe that he had really enjoyed his time in the police force.

The different characteristics and qualities of my Dartford colleagues became of interest to me. I had never worked in such a mixed environment with so much contact with so many different people. Recollections of these fellow workers bring a warm feeling and an inner smile.

Senior on my section was Colin. He had served earlier in the British Army but had never mentioned to any of his present colleagues what he had got up to against the Hun. Such was the way with the ex-armed forces officers. His actions were always considered first and carried out with deliberation. He never got excited or harassed but took things in his stride and was a great example to the younger constables. Strangely, he never partook in the morning tea break. Instead, he always made his own extraordinary brew in his ex-army billycan. Whilst the water was boiling, he emptied about half a packet of tea into the can, which he then infused by pouring the boiling water halfway up the can. He then topped up the contents from a tin of condensed milk. Some 4-5 spoons of sugar were ladled into the liquid and stirred for a minute or so.

The resulting concoction was so thick, the teaspoon almost stood up in it. Apparently, he had always brewed this way and continued to do so for as long as I knew him. No-one ever asked Colin to "Make the tea" for our section.

Ken was the gaoler. Another ex-forces type approaching his retirement, he had landed the plum job as full-time gaoler. The advantage of this position was a steady 7am to 3pm shift, Monday to Friday, with overtime when the court sat late and there were prisoners to sort out—which was most days.

Working with Ken, I was to learn the best way to deal with all sorts of miscreant, from the armed robber to the simple drunk. No-one enjoys having the door slammed behind them, especially when it was within the confines of a Dartford police cell in the early 1960s!

The cell was about 12 feet long by 6 feet wide. It was entered through a great wooden door engraved with nearly 100 years of prisoners' graffiti, and at the far end was a high, small, barred window to provide a glimmer of light. The floor was concrete and the walls were of some type of grey wash that had last been treated before the war.

Towards the end of my service at Dartford, the entire police station was re-decorated, for the first time in many years, with a strange pneumatic device that sprayed spots of different colours onto a white base. That went onto every interior wall in the building, including the cell walls, and the furniture and floor in some places.

There was a very rudimentary toilet bowl in each cell, flushed from a cistern in the outer passage. If a prisoner requested a blanket for his palliasse he was given one—provided there were no more than 6 prisoners in residence!

I feel that I should describe the palliasse for those who are unaware of the item. At Dartford police station cells, there was a store room at the end of the cell passage that contained the rudimentary requirements of inmates. A hand-written sign on the door sarcastically displayed the words, "Prisoner Care".

Amongst these items were the palliasses. They were canvas sacks, roughly the size of a small single mattress, stuffed with a mixture of straw and horse hair. The horse hair, being rather rare, not to say, old, had collapsed over the years and was bolstered by the addition of more readily available straw from local suppliers. This addition enlarged the item to a size that could accommodate a sleeping man.

Whether they were ever cleaned in any way is unknown—the original colour having greyed over so many years of use.

It was one of Ken's jobs to keep the cells clean, which he called "fluffing up the mattresses".

There was a shelf above the pile of palliasses which held the other requisites necessary for completion of the "Prisoner Care" package: A tooth brush of unknown provenance, a small bar of soap and a face cloth of dubious origin. Obviously, the provision of razors was banned. We had "Health & Safety" rules, even in those days.

To my knowledge, Ken only fell foul of authority once, and that was a major event. Three armed robbers had been placed in the cells, pending their appearance at the courthouse, at the same time that many other prisoners had been remanded to the cells, meaning that there was a degree of overcrowding and Ken was under severe pressure to keep up with the calls demanded of him from the magistrates' court next door. In the course of transferring the prisoners, Ken failed to check behind the open door behind which one of the robbers had hidden.

At that time, there were no secondary gates in the cell passageway and the man was able to simply walk into the passage and away before he was missed. How the powers that be could accept that one elderly police constable could maintain security of nearly a dozen prisoners on his own whilst transferring them between the cells and the courthouse is astonishing, but Ken was put on a Number One (discipline report) for that.

Within the Dartford police area were a number of hospitals and mental institutions, all of which had their fair share of death reports. The majority of these required a Coroner's Inquest to determine the cause of death before any funeral proceedings could take place and to facilitate the necessary chain of events between death and inquest, an officer, entitled "Coroner's Officer" was appointed to specialise in those investigations and do all the bidding of his coroner.

Brian was our Coroner's Officer and he had his own small office at Dartford Police Station from where he spent all hours of the day attending deaths, arranging for the removal of bodies to the mortuary, setting up the post mortem examinations and reporting the findings to the coroner for his decision.

When regular officers were obliged to attend venues of sudden deaths, they were expected to confer with Brian regarding completion of the requisite "Blue" forms and he ensured that there was control and consistency over all death reports passing through his office. Brian also arranged for local undertakers to liaise with relatives with a view to catering for the cremation or burial of the deceased. As such, he had a very close working relationship with those local undertakers and he drove round in a luxurious Rover saloon car.

He was a remarkably efficient and knowledgeable man who probably did the work of ten civilians today.

Experience has its rewards and he was an example to all those employees who wish to build their own empire within a wider organisation so that they are regarded as totally irreplaceable.

Every day, all section members reported for duty in the parade room fifteen minutes before the appointed hour when duty was to be commenced.

There was to be no payment forthcoming for these fifteen minute periods spent around the table before official duty commenced. It was just one of those things that was done.

One bright spark worked out that, if he added all the additional fifteen minutes parading time together, after a year he would have worked more than one week in actual unpaid time. He sought the support of the Police Federation in getting an extra week's holiday in lieu of that time but it was never going to work.

Officers sat round the huge heavy table and the latest entries from the Occurrence Book were read out by the duty sergeant, followed by excerpts from the crime book and other local orders.

Beats were then allocated and specific duties given. In addition, all officers were expected to study the thick folder containing the latest copies of The Police Gazette.

This publication had been in print ever since 1840 and was a UK-wide paper sent to every police station describing the persons suspected of serious crime, with their full descriptions and other information. Even in 1962, 120 or so years on, it still contained valid and active information for assimilation by the patrolling police officer but has now been superseded by the Police Nation Computer in all its forms and indices.

All orders having been given and received, the section was ready to exit onto the street at the appointed hour. There was no ceremony, simply because there was just not enough time.

Less busy police stations in the country insisted upon something called accoutrement parade. This is where the section of men stands in a line in full uniform and receives their instructions instead of, like us, sitting down around a table with a smoking cigarette.

Where parades took place, the sergeant or duty inspector called the men to attention and issued the order, "Accoutrements". The men then had to form a line at attention and produce their truncheon, handcuffs and pocketbook for inspection. This was then followed by a formal "Dismiss", a smart salute to the front and a 90 degree turn to the right. All this was an obvious throwback to earlier days of policing when there was a strong Armed Services influence. We had gone through the motions of accoutrement parade at the training centre with Sergeant Sellars so we were expecting this sort of regimentation, but Dartford policing rarely allowed time for such indulgences.

Many times, a call would be received before our duty period began, when the entire section would grab their helmets and coats to go to some serious incident or attend a call for assistance to help a colleague.

During the summer of 1963, a strict and rather young new inspector arrived at Dartford—probably a punishment posting for some domestic misdemeanour, we thought—and he attempted to apply the Accoutrements Parade on an occasion when manpower and time were in particularly short supply. I think that his previous posting had been at some quiet town with sufficient officers who would willingly participate in such dated formalities.

There were only four constables sitting around our parade-room table in preparation for the shifts instruction when Sergeant. Wills came in to warn us that the new inspector had ordered that we were to have "one of those formal parades". Of the four of us, Mick was blessed with a physically large head. He was probably issued with the largest size of helmet ever made for the British bobby. Whereas Eric, a tall, lanky officer with nearly 30 years service and a distinguished war record, had an exceedingly small head and, at the other end of the spectrum, had been issued with a correspondingly tiny helmet.

The expected order was shouted by the new inspector as he entered the parade room and we four reluctant officers got up and stood in a line, tunics buttoned and helmets on heads—except that Eric and Mick had swapped headgear. The helmet on Eric's head came over his head, completely covering his eyes and ears, almost down to his shoulders, whilst Mick looked as if he was wearing a party hat and only needed a coloured party blower and big red nose to complete the comedy ensemble.

All four of us managed to keep a straight face, although Heaven knows how. This irreverent episode caused the inspector to stand in disbelief at this outrageous disregard of discipline, and for the formality of the occasion. There were several seconds of total stunned silence whilst his face changed to a bright red colour and the ends of his mouth started to twitch. He suddenly dissolved into paroxysms of laughter; with the result that he never attempted to impose such formal parades upon us again.

Being "Late on Parade" was a worry for me. I have always been one who enjoys the warmth of a comfortable bed, and nothing is more comfortable than your own bed at 5.00am on a February morning! Especially comfortable if the dawning day is cold, wet, or both. The struggle into work was a necessary evil if a young officer was to avoid the threat of a Number 8.

Regulation 8 of Police Regulations used to allow a police force to dismiss an unsuitable officer at any time during his two year probationary period without appeal if his behaviour is deemed lacking in the essential ways. I don't think modern employment law would allow such actions.

Apart from dear Mrs Whitehead, who later suffered from cataracts of the eyes and had to give up taking lodgers, I had digs in 1964 with another kindly lady on the other side of town who cared for my domestic needs up until the time I was married. From both of these landladies, I had to borrow a large saucepan whenever I was on early turn. Before retiring at night, I set my enormous double-belled alarm clock and placed it inside the saucepan, well out of reach of the flailing arm of a semi-conscious sleepyhead.

It worked most times; with the additional reliance upon the landlady for a screamed "Are you up yet!" to finally wake up. In those days, there was no house telephone to use to make late excuses to the early-turn sergeant, such as having gone down with an attack of boils, dysentery, childbirth or a mixture of any of those during the night. It was not unknown that, for some consideration (clean the windows, paint the back door, etc.) the landlady would walk down the road in her robe and slippers to the local telephone box at 6am to report that her poor lodger had a very high temperature and couldn't come to work that day. Problem here was one had then to take all three days off for the sake of the authenticity of uncertificated sick leave.

A colleague, Derek, was the most fortunate officer at the nick. His main claim to fame was that he originated from Bethnal Green, in east London, and had gone to Daniel Street School with the notorious Kray brothers just after the war.

He and his wife enjoyed the comfort of having their apartment actually above the police station. There was living accommodation available above the north side of the building, directly over the parade room area. Access was via a door located behind the officers' lockers.

Derek and I were frequently on the same shift and my first duty on arrival for early turn was to check that he was up. Many were the times that he appeared for morning parade, bleary-eyed, with no collar or tie, with a cup of coffee in his hand.

Once, he really tried it on by coming down to the parade room in his pyjamas, but Sergeant Wills drew the line there.

One illustration of the many unwritten solutions to making a busy nick work with too few officers was the serving of Court Warrants.

Dartford had more than its share of law-breakers and defaulters living amongst us, and the Warrants Folder in the front office was always rather fat. It seemed that as fast as attempts were made to reduce the backlog, additions from the court office made sure that an empty folder was never to be achieved.

Normally, two officers with four-wheeled transport would attend the address, arrest the defaulter, convey him to the police station where he would be processed and probably bailed to appear before the Bench; then go out and get another one by way of the same procedure. It was a rather long-winded and time-consuming exercise.

The station transport accessible to us included the 999 van (the aforementioned Austin A60), the inspector's old black Hillman Minx saloon—which he usually wanted so that he could go home for his dinner or any other non-official purpose which that senior officer deemed essential at the time—and the CID's even older and tattier Hillman Minx van. Also available were two ancient Velocette Li 150cc water-cooled motorcycles and several privately-owned pedal cycles in the back shed. There was the large, dark blue prison van but hardly anyone was qualified to drive that. It was a few years old and was already displaying signs of rust yet it hadn't even done 5,000 miles.

The logistics of effective warrant clearing were thus considered. The answers were multiple.

(A) Use the 999 car and hope that an emergency call would not be received whilst the crew was conveying a defaulter. It was not unknown for an arrested person to have to accompany the arresting officer to an emergency incident before the opportunity was available to complete the original journey. One such miscreant volunteered to direct traffic around a particularly messy accident whilst caught up in such a problem and very good at it he was too.

(B) Send the sub-divisional motorcyclist on his Velocette to the defaulter's home to instruct the subject to present himself to the police station as soon as possible. You may think that this would never work, but the threat of having the night duty turn up at 3.00am and waking the whole street up if the subject failed to comply was frequently a sufficient inducement.

(C) Telephone the offender and use the same argument as (B). This was a rarely used method as most households didn't have a telephone. Most didn't have a doorbell, either! That is why police officers were issued truncheons—with which to knock on the front doors.

Even if there was only 50% success in carrying out these possibilities, it was amazing how quickly the thickness of the warrant file diminished.

On some days, the personnel carrier did become available to us and that eased the problem even more. Two officers would work out an early morning route to include as many defaulters' addresses as possible. They would go from house to house collecting the prisoners with the promise that they would be returned in the same order at the end of the morning.

Arriving back at the nick with up to eight prisoners for processing all at once really did get the duty sergeant very tetchy.

Of course, there were the more difficult customers to deal with, especially those with warrants marked "No Bail". This endorsement meant that when the police finally "collared" the prisoner, he was to be documented at the police station and then conveyed straight away to Her Majesties Prison to be incarcerated for the stipulated period of time. This could range from seven days to whatever the courts had ordered; months, if need be. For an easier life, the arrest was made to avoid any commitments the defaulter might have—within reason.

Rarely were problems encountered or friction increased between the Force and the residents of the town because good humour and levity were tools of our trade. The prisoners were simply carted off to Canterbury prison and left in the care of the prison authorities until they were due for release.

As I mentioned earlier, the magistrates' court was located to the rear of the police station and all prisoners who were either convicted or remanded in custody were secured in the police station cells until they could be transferred to the appropriate secure accommodation (prison).

Generally, that transfer was carried out by using the personnel carrier driven by a civilian driver, if there was one available, with a uniformed escort who was responsible for the prisoners property, the appropriate warrant and the thick book known as the Body Book for which a written receipt was received from the receiving authority on safe delivery of the prisoner.

On arrival at the prison, the police vehicle was permitted to enter the gates and the prisoner was escorted to the prisoner reception area for handing over to the prison officers.

These escort duties were a favoured assignment as it meant several hours away from the town routine and invariably a quiet cup of tea on the way home.

It was also a frequent event for a juvenile offender to be sent to a remand centre for the attempts to be made to reform him. From Dartford, the usual destination was to escort him to Ashford (Middlesex) Remand Centre, which was renowned for its strict discipline.

Escorts of this type were carried out by public transport and entailed getting two railway warrants made out for the journey, exchangeable for tickets at the railway booking office.

The offender was then handcuffed to the escorting police officer and taken in the police car to Dartford railway station where the railway warrant was processed. The train to London Waterloo station was then boarded.

At Waterloo, prisoner and escort transferred to Waterloo mainline station where the train to Ashford was boarded.

On reaching Ashford, it was then a one mile walk to the remand centre for the offender to be admitted at reception. In this modern day, such journeys are undertaken by specialist civilian companies in totally secure mobile cells. The chances of problems en route in the 1960s were rather high.

One day, it was my turn to bolster the overtime pay and do escort duty to the remand centre. I organised the railway warrant, got the necessary property and paperwork together in the property bag and handcuffed the young man to my left wrist.

He was very nervous, having just received his first custodial sentence and was on the verge of tears. I had actually had previous dealings with this lad and had not considered him any danger; merely that he liked other people's possessions too much.

I had released the handbolts before Waterloo with the solemn warning that woe betide him if he tried to run. He assured me that he would behave and he kept his word through the concourse of Waterloo station, giving me no problems whatsoever. I was even generous enough to buy us both a cup of tea at the tea stand by the entrance to the station, which is now an expensive coffee bar.

We caught the onward train to Ashford where we came out of the railway station onto the public road—when he suddenly sprinted off.

The problem for him was that he was running along the route that led to the remand centre. I was also quite fit and was able to keep up with him quite easily—and I have to say that I was not exactly happy that he had made off from me. So much for trust.

I then saw, ahead of him, two tall mature men walking towards us who had obviously seen the two of us running at some considerable speed along the pavement; me with my civilian coat open showing my uniform beneath it. They parted to allow the lad to pass between them and, as he did so, lifted him off his feet and then onto the ground, face down.

I reached the group and one of the men said to me, "We are from the remand centre. We will help you march him down there." I replaced the handbolts, feeling rather stupid that I had offered my trust to the little scoundrel, and we arrived at reception a few minutes later, where he received the usual welcome from the stern reception officer.

This was the day that I realised that you do not indulge any convicted offender with excessive respect, politeness or humour.

On another similar escort to Ashford, I had a young man who considered that life at Ashford Remand Centre would be a bed of roses. Throughout the journey, where he remained firmly handcuffed to me all the way, he was bragging to me about how tough he was and that the "screws" couldn't do anything to wind him up.

I merely advised him to be respectful to the reception officer. That he must stand to attention at the desk. He must call him "Sir" after every question, and only speak when spoken to. On giving this advice, all I got back was a stream of rude words. He obviously considered himself to be a big man and no-one was going to order him about.

On arrival at the reception office, we walked up to the imposing desk, behind which stood a tall uniformed prison officer of strict military appearance. I removed the handcuffs and placed the warrant, body book and prisoner's property onto the desk top. I addressed the reception officer formally, gave the name of the young lad and outlined the sentence handed down by the magistrates and stepped back several paces.

The officer picked up the paperwork and studied it, followed by a question to the young man to which he did not receive a satisfactory reply. I took another step back. Further questions were barked at the lad and he reacted by smiling! Not once had the lad said "Sir". Nor had he shown any respect whatsoever for this prison officer.

My prudence in taking several steps back were proved justified, because in an instant, the prison officer came round the desk and smacked the lad hard around his face, causing him to sprawl across the office.

Within a few minutes, this miscreant was saying "Sir" so many times, I was convinced that he now had the message. The lad caught my eye and I could see his tears welling up. I smiled back and left to get the train home.

It was several months later that our paths crossed in Dartford High Street following his release from the remand centre. I have to say that he was a changed man. He even showed me respect and admitted that he had been foolish not to listen to my advice. I asked him how long before his face had returned to its correct colour. He smiled at me and said "A few days".

I honestly believe that he learned, that opening day, that it might be easier to conform to authority rather than go hard against it.

CHAPTER 4

Taking a Light View of Policing

FOR RELAXATION, IN common with a lot of police stations in Kent, a tiny licensed bar was located on the top floor of Dartford police station. Such facilities are frowned upon these days and the Police Station Club is now a very rare establishment. I mean, it is wrong for officers to consort with their friends and colleagues where there is the temptation of alcohol—isn't it?

Our small bar-room only had space for four tables with chairs, as well as a couple of bar stools in front of the serving hatch. Two or three members of the elected bar-committee worked a rota to open the bar and dispense Watney's Red Barrel, or a measure of spirits from the limited selection available.

Through the door alongside the hatch, was access to the inner sanctum, or billiard room, where stood an ancient full-sized snooker table in pristine condition. It must have been over 60 years old. Elevated seats were built around the walls with, at the end of the room, an antique mahogany snooker scoreboard, complete with a revolving rack for the members' cues. There was a pervading odour of ancient cigar smoke and floor polish, and it was like stepping back into the days of Joe Davis and Walter Lindrum.

Whilst playing on this beautifully true table, illuminated only by the three 150watt bulbs hanging from the large, deep red, fabric shade above, one could imagine being in an important tournament and challenging the world's best player.

The truth of it all was less impressive. However, practice helped (but didn't make perfect!) and I took a playing interest in the game of snooker and participated in our local force tournaments for many years. There is little doubt that a frame or two of snooker has a very therapeutic effect especially if it follows a late shift dealing with domestic violence, rowdy drunks and crazy drivers.

Alas, there are not many snooker tables at police stations these days. Too many civilians and administrative staff need their offices.

For a young single policeman who nearly always patrolled alone, apart from the initial familiarisation period, the police station bar and billiard room were the places where new friends were made, stories exchanged, and the skills of snooker and billiards honed.

Some tales were subject to exaggeration, but a couple of my favourites involved an ancient constable named Joseph whose primary task was to man the front desk.

One afternoon, a well-dressed and well-spoken gentleman entered the front office and demanded to speak with the chief inspector regarding a confidential matter. Joseph enquired whether the man had an appointment but the answer was that he did not. Joseph then went to the chief inspector and asked him whether or not he could speak with the caller, to which the chief agreed. Joseph then said, "By the way, sir. The gentleman is extremely deaf and speaks with a very loud voice." Joseph then returned to the front desk to show the man through to the office and, on the way, said to the caller, "I have to warn you, sir, that the chief inspector is an extremely deaf man and speaks in a very loud voice".

Thus, Joseph was later able to convey the contents of that confidential meeting to anyone who cared to enquire.

It was also Joseph who was responsible for the American newspapers circulating and printing a story about the Great Straw Storm of Dartford in 1963.

That August, following a rather hot period when harvesting was underway in the fields behind the Fleet estate, there came a series of small dust devils, or air vortexes caused by the hot dry conditions. As the dust devils crossed the field, some of the cut straw was lifted high into the clear blue sky, carried towards the estate where the vortexes died and the airborne straw fell to ground on the roads and gardens of the estate.

The local paper was a bit short of news that week and it included a piece of exaggerated copy, indicating that the amount of straw blown in the vortexes was rather more than had actually occurred.

The following day Joseph was on duty at the station switchboard when he received a telephone call from a rather naïve correspondent at an American news agency based in New York who had somehow heard about the news item and now wished to have confirmation of this strange phenomenon from an official source; hence his call to an English police station.

Joseph was many things, but an official source was not one to which he had ever staked his claim. However, he jumped at the chance of being an "official police spokesman" in this case, and vividly described to the eager newsman the astonishing scene of the whirlwind's aftermath with scores of English peasants in their embroidered smocks, driving their carthorses and armed with pitchforks, going to the aid of people who were buried up to their necks in the stuff, and then making stooks of straw in readiness for the winter.

We never heard what was put into print for the American readership to feast on the following morning, but the story always brought a smile of enjoyment to our faces.

Although police cars were equipped with radio apparatus to facilitate contact between headquarters and car crew, personal radios were not issued to individual officers in Kent until 1968.

Up until then, whenever a foot policeman left the police station to go on patrol, he would not be contactable and was responsible for his own actions. To get round this problem, foot patrols were required to be at specific locations at pre-designated times in order that they could receive any messages from the local controlling office.

These locations, or "points" as they were known, were decided on by the sergeant at parade, and were usually at designated telephone kiosks, but could as easily be shops or other premises where the appearance of a uniformed officer would be accepted as normal.

In Dartford most points were at telephone kiosks which, in addition to a telephone, provided a degree of shelter when the weather was inclement.

The duration of the point was usually fifteen minutes, followed by a 45 minute period to allow the patrolling officer to make his own route across his allocated beat to the next point.

Should there be matters affecting that patrol, the officer would hear the telephone ring and receive the necessary orders.

The sergeant was also aware of the location of the officer so that he could join him at the telephone kiosk to sign his pocket book.

Senior officers could also be expected to make surprise visits when they had little else better to do.

Almost every new policeman was set up to be a "Patsy" for the favourite wind-up. It would probably be late evening when the young probationer was standing in the High Street by a telephone kiosk, waiting to get away to his next warm cup of tea.

The telephone would ring and the officer pick up the receiver and acknowledge the call, "Hello, Pc Plod here." A voice at the other end of the line would announce that it was the duty inspector speaking and apologise for not being able to get down and meet at the point personally. Meanwhile, was everything quiet in the town? The young officer, over-awed by receiving a telephone call from a senior officer, would report "All correct, sir." The caller would then ask whether the officer was in possession of all his accoutrements, to which the constable would answer in the affirmative. Next the caller requested evidence that the constable was correctly equipped and asked to hear the rap of the truncheon on the handset. This was duly performed. Next, a request to have the hand bolts rattled at the mouthpiece. Again, this was complied with. Finally, the whistle was to be blown.

By this time, the young constable would feel that he was being made an idiot of—but could he be sure? That is the secret of a good wind-up. You can never be sure if the request is genuine because so many requests from senior officers can seem so petty.

The truth was frequently revealed when other members of the shift would appear outside the kiosk to jeer the poor fool who had been standing rattling his hand bolts into a public telephone mouthpiece.

A scheduled early practical experience was to witness a *post mortem* examination at the West Hill Hospital. Much of the police officer's duty time is spent in matters connected with the death of someone or other, so the matter of getting used to this was considered important from the earliest point in the officer's career.

In common with many young men of my age, I had never had to experience looking at a dead body. So it was that three of us were detailed to meet with the mortician at West Hill Mortuary.

In the United Kingdom a doctor is allowed to issue a death certificate if he can be certain what the cause of death of an individual actually was, and that it was due to natural causes. All this being subject to other rules determining such things as the last time the doctor examined the deceased, etc.

In every other case the Coroner has to issue a death certificate based on the cause of death which has been determined by a pathologist at a formal post mortem.

In most cases the cause of death is found to have been due to natural causes, such as a heart attack or stroke. In other cases the deceased may have been involved in an accident, or violent death, which can be established by the pathologist in the course of his examination of the entire body.

In a post mortem every part of the body is examined to ensure that nothing is missed, with samples frequently taken and retained for later pathology.

The police officer has an important role to play in providing continuous evidence of identification from the time of death to the Coroner's Inquest. He has to be present and witness a lot of post mortem examinations, many of which are not very pleasant. The first p.m. is therefore the most important.

So to West Hill Hospital. The mortician at such an establishment is usually a man of many years experience who, whilst reverent in the presence of family or senior medical staff, is completely the opposite when working at his grim task in the privacy of the mortuary. Like undertakers, morticians have a wonderfully black sense of humour.

Similarly, such medical pathologists in general hospitals are experts in establishing death but show little outward concern for the cadaver if only professionals are present. To such men, policemen are professional, regardless of age or experience. My first view of a post mortem examination was to remain in my memory forever.

The West Hill mortuary was a large room, with no natural light, in the bowels of the hospital. The first thing to hit the senses was the very strong smell of medical cleaning fluid and disinfectant. On one side was a wall containing several stainless steel drawers—deep ones—for holding bodies. A system of rollers allowed the body to be moved from the steel drawer onto a gurney and trundled across the floor of the mortuary to the examination table. This table was made of stainless steel and was kept spotlessly clean.

On this particular day the radio was tuned into the Light Programme and playing "I Like It" by Gerry and the Pacemakers.

The subject of this performance in the art of opening up a deceased person was an elderly male who had passed away on the ward of a geriatric unit at Stone Hospital. For some reason the man's doctor was unable to give a certain cause of death, hence the need for the post mortem examination.

When we arrived Stan, the mortician, had unshrouded the body to reveal a well-built eighty-year-old. Stan explained to Philip, Mike and me that it was his job to prepare the body for the pathologist. This required him to "remove the lid" and open up the thorax. This was done by seemingly scalping the man from the back of the head and pulling the scalp over the front of the face. This revealed the bone of the scull which was then removed as if taking the top off an egg. A scalpel cut was made from the neck, straight down to the top of the groin, revealing the rib cage, which was then cut away using long-handled pruning shears, thus revealing the man's vital organs.

Stan performed this operation in only a couple of minutes and I could see that Phil was not a happy person. The colour had totally drained from his face and he was swaying slightly—not a good sign for a hard copper.

Enter the pathologist who greeted us in his usual cheery manner and proceeded to get down to what he did best, delving away inside the chest cavity and withdrawing the lungs and heart. He then snipped away in the red mess and pulled the bowels and liver out with a flourish. These items were placed on the dissecting table, with some organs being passed to us for weighing and noting.

He talked throughout, giving us great detail on what he was doing. Phil grasped the table behind him and his eyes seemed to lose focus.

Finally there was the examination of the lung tissue where the cause of death was suspected to be found. The pathologist held a lung in one hand and drew a long knife through the tissue with the other. He squeezed the lung between his hands and it seemed that lots of grey worms exuded from the red tissue.

Phil changed his position from vertical to horizontal and went to sleep for a few minutes. "Pneumonia," exclaimed the pathologist. "Sew him up, Stan, and we can have a cup of tea before the next one."

It took a long time for Phil to recover from that first post mortem examination and, indeed, it was to be his last. It turned out that he had a weakness in these less savoury areas of police work and he decided to go and work for the railway instead. I have to admit that I found the entire medical examination absorbing and when having to attend such examinations I have always taken a considerable interest in the science of the pathologist.

Retaining such an attitude, it is possible to treat a dead body encountered in the course of duty as an impersonal entity and not to become emotionally involved with the more tragic areas that may have been the cause of the death, but never to show this lack of personal care when in the presence of relatives or other persons having a special interest.

CHAPTER 5

Looking to Gain Experience.

DURING THE FIRST three months of foot patrol in the first new town following training, it was regarded as necessary for all probationary constables to have a tutor constable accompany them. Whilst this did not always happen, especially at such a busy place as Dartford, each station had a number of officers considered by the senior staff to have the necessary experience to pass good advice to the new bloods. In this way the probationer would learn the art of being an effective policeman by the example of the older man, and also be kept on a tight rein to prevent too many foolish decisions being made. It is all very well having legislation drummed into the head but to be a respected and effective police officer, a practical knowledge of life, together with the ability to recognise the standing of persons within the class structure, was considered to be of vital importance.

Back in the 1960s, like most towns, Dartford had a few old coppers for whom progress through the ranks was beyond their personal strengths.

Most were ex-services, de-mobs and short service retirees who had embarked upon a life of being a policeman because it was a convenient and useful profession in Civvy Street. Some of these were men who had fought in the war in Europe and beyond and had learned their discipline in the Armed Forces. Academically, they were perhaps not as fluent as the modern recruit, but what knowledge they lacked of law books, they made up for with good common sense and reasoning.

Regrettably, such men do not appear to be evident in today's police force where individualism and the ability to think for oneself seem to be less important than being a team member.

And so back to Jack who was the first friendly policeman I had ever met, when he greeted me upon my arrival at Dartford Police Station.

Jack was an ex-army, non-commissioned officer and had served in the Far East. Like men of his character, he was unwilling to detail many events that he had witnessed or even endured whilst serving King and Country in the war, but without any doubt, those experiences had created a man who commanded huge respect from his peers. He had a quiet and unassuming manner which seemed to give his colleagues indefinable support. He was well over six feet in height with a broad chest, but had a comportment which could be described as reverential.

Jack was to be my tutor constable but, because of duty commitments, the best plans of the chief inspector rarely come to fruition. Frequently, because of conflicting duty, sickness, training courses and annual leave the teaming up of tutor with pupil could not always be achieved and, like many young officers, I had to fend for myself when the tutor was on other duties, or called away.

Certainly, the chief inspector wanted ALL his men on the streets, where they were deemed to be effective, even if it meant that a new lad, wet behind the ears, could go it alone in a domestic situation or whatever else he might be called upon to attend.

I knew that being in company with Jack wherever possible would provide a good grounding for my future as a copper and I looked forward to my opportunities to accompany him around the town.

One weekday, just after the lunchtime session in the pubs, Jack and I found ourselves on foot patrol in Dartford High Street, when a customer of The Bull public house came up to us to report that the landlord was having a problem with another customer. Not the strangest of events in Dartford. Jack led the way into the saloon bar of the premises which was empty apart from a middle-aged man, very much inebriated, seated on the bar stool against the far wall. We were greeted in the usual fashion, which included much invective.

The landlord appeared pleased to see us and told us that he was trying to close the pub and that the customer had refused to leave.

Broken glass was strewn around the floor and on the bar, apparently created by the inebriate, especially so given the broken neck of a bottle still in his hand.

"Have you requested him to leave?" asked Jack.

"Of course I have. That's what set him off," said the landlord.

"Well, we can't do your work for you. You got him drunk so you throw him out," said Jack.

"If I try and throw him out, he'll smash something else," said the landlord.

"We will assist you to eject him, landlord. We will not do it for you."

The landlord again asked the man to leave and received a string of threats, accompanied by the usual adjectives.

"You see," said the landlord, "He won't go. You will have to eject him".

"We cannot help unless you make a physical attempt to eject him," repeated Jack.

With that, the landlord came around to the main bar and laid a hand on the drunk in a vain effort to pull him off his stool. The drunk swore and took a swing at the landlord with the broken bottle in his fist.

Immediately, Jack moved with the speed of a cobra striking. He grabbed the drunken man by the hair and ran him across the floor of the bar to the front door. The drunk was then hurled out of the door and fetched up on the pavement in a dazed heap, with passers-by aghast at this sudden intrusion to their shopping.

"There," said Jack quietly to the landlord, "We won't do your work for you, but we will give you the necessary assistance. I suggest you don't put profit before safety again. An entry will be inserted in the Licensed Premises Register".

Lesson learned for the next thirty years. An officer is permitted to assist the licensee, but never do all the work on private premises himself.

Such was the surprise of the drunk that after he was invited to "Go home quietly", he complied and actually apologised for his actions. You don't see that today.

Mistakes; I've made a few. Especially on night duty, when most interesting things seemed to happen to me.

One of the duties we had was the checking of unoccupied homes whilst the owners were away on holiday. Each "Beat Tray" contained the list of each house visited and the time and date recorded. I was on Stone beat and collected the list for Stone, which, I have to say in my defence, was an area unlit by street lights and not familiar to me.

Three o'clock on a dark, damp morning saw me in Church Lane at Stone, searching for 2 Church Lane Cottages, which appeared, in the gloom, to be at the end of the lane (near the church, obviously). I duly found the cottage with "2" on the door and walked around the garden. The window at the back was broken and when I tried the back door, it was unlocked. Hmmm. Better let the sergeant know before taking this any further. I had already been in trouble for taking action on my own before and so prudence was my watchword.

I walked up to the main road and telephoned the police station and waited for the car to come.

In ten minutes the duty sergeant arrived with another officer and I took them down to number 2 and round the back. "Good lad", said Sergeant Milner, "Looks like you found a break-in."

We entered the kitchen and spread out through the house. Sergeant Milner went upstairs and there was then a blood-tingling scream. I fear that Sergeant Milner had entered the bedroom of the occupiers and the lady had awoken to find a man standing over her with his torch!

It seems that this dwelling was 2 Church Cottages and not 2 Church Lane Cottages, which was even further down the lane and, as it turned out, very secure. Sergeant Milner never forgave me for that one.

Some of the tasks required of a constable are less than enjoyable, such as passing on the news of sudden death. My first ever "Death Message" was detailed to me during an early shift; I having just finished my breakfast in the kitchen. It was to be one detail that I shall always remember.

With no women police officers on duty and no-one else being available with a pedal cycle, I was instructed by the duty sergeant to make my way to Temple Hill Estate where I was to inform a lady that her husband had been crushed to death on a construction site at nearby Erith where he worked.

As it was to be my first such message delivery, I was given some brief verbal advice by the sergeant, which included the suggestion that I make a call upon a neighbouring resident first to seek out a female companion who might be willing to accompany me.

I arrived in the road where the lady lived and called at the next-door neighbour's house where the female occupant who answered the bell listened to my request and promptly burst into tears.

She recovered sufficiently to tell me that she had known the deceased and his wife quite well. Because of her near-hysterical condition, she declined to accompany me next door but said that she would put the kettle on for a cup of tea for me (why not the widow as well?). She shut the front door and left me to it.

I rang the soon-to-be-notified-widow's door bell several times before I heard movement and the door was then answered by a very attractive young lady with short blonde hair.

She was still wearing night attire and it left little to my young man's imagination. She smiled at me on seeing that it was a young bright-eyed uniformed policeman who was calling.

The vision in front of me, together with the sad purpose of my visit, made me tremble with uncertainty.

I identified myself and she confirmed that she was, indeed, the wife of the building-site worker, the subject of my call. She invited me to come into the front room where I, with little hesitation, merely blurted out to her, "I have to inform you that your husband is dead. He was killed on the building site this morning. I am very sorry."

I stood and waited for the expected histrionics. All she said was, "Oh, really? Well that will save the expense of a solicitor. We were going to get a divorce soon." Several moments of uncertain silence passed before I said, "Would you like a cup of tea? The lady next door is putting the kettle on." To which she replied, "Not with that bitch. She is the cause of it all!"

Thus, her neighbour's tears and response to the news were also explained.

The nice blonde lady then made coffee for the two of us whilst I explained what she was now required to do, and what we could do for her to assist with later identification and other formal matters.

Her demeanour showed that she was less interested in the death of her husband and rather more interested in a 19-year-old uniformed policeman.

It is the truth that I left the house before I had finished the cup of coffee. Everything else remained untouched—including the biscuits.

I encountered more problems with the opposite sex at 3am one morning whilst making a "point" at a telephone kiosk in a better area of Dartford.

As usual for this time of night, it was very quiet and I had shaken hands with countless door handles in my quest to find an insecurity which normally meant a theoretical bonus point from the sergeant.

I was actually standing in the kiosk writing in my pocketbook when the door opened and a middle-aged woman stood there wearing only a wrap around her body and with a worried look on her face. "Oh! Am I glad I have found a policeman," she said. "My daughter is going to have a baby and I have to call the midwife. Would you pop into number 36 across the road and see if she is still OK whilst I see if I can get through to the nurse."

Recognising a genuine case where help was expected, even from a copper still wet behind the ears, I made my way across the road and into number 36 where the front door was open and the lights were all on.

I heard myself call out "Hallo?" and was answered by a ladies strained voice from the front room.

On entering I was faced with the soon-to-be young mother, lying on the carpet with her knees in the air and dressed in rather less than her mother. "What do you want me to do?" I asked. Any recollection of first aid training had deserted me, apart from the need to provide plenty of hot water, but she did not want me to leave her alone.

I believe I did all the right things and remained with her whilst waiting for medical assistance to arrive—which it did, just in time. It was a lovely baby boy.

Why was I scheduled for night duty on March 17th every year? St Patrick's Day inevitably becomes the night that the Irish tend to celebrate with even more gusto than every other night spent with Mr Guinness or Mr Murphy, and creates alcohol-related incidents in which I frequently seemed to get involved.

In the early 1960s the construction of the first Dartford tunnel was continuing apace. A great number of the construction crews were of Irish descent and many lodged in Dartford.

The Irish Club, in Lowfield Street, was a particularly popular venue for the Irish workers and a place where their Friday night intellectual discourse on the causes of the Cold War and other issues of international significance were reduced to base physical, alcohol-fuelled disagreement. At closing time a series of calls used to be received from residents living in the vicinity of the club, complaining of large groups of men spilling out of the club and fighting in the street.

The location was only some 2 minutes from the police station but, invariably, we took at least 10 minutes to respond to the calls. First, by then, they would have punched themselves silly and were ready to go home, and second, there were rarely more than three night-duty officers available to attend. Imagine the problems we would have had if we had arrived when the fight was still in its best stages. No. Get there late and tell them politely to go home. No trouble with them at all, at all.

Most inebriated Irishmen still kept a modicum of respect for policemen in those days. It was not always the case, as demonstrated on St Patrick's Night 1964.

I was on my own, walking the beat, at around 12.30am in Dartford High Street. From my position in a doorway I saw two men making their stout-fuelled way along the street when they came to where the potato-chip delivery man had left a large polythene bag full of 28 pounds weight of raw chipped potatoes by the door of a café, ready for the next day's business.

Goods used to be left outside such premises with little chance of damage or theft because the majority of people back then would not have interfered with them. However, these two men thought it would be funny to pick up the bag and use it as a rugby ball. It held for the first few passes and then burst open, showering the street with raw chips.

I moved forward and apprehended them for causing criminal damage. Me, 20-years-old, eleven stone and baby faced, arresting two full grown, drunken Irishmen who had spent the last few months moving vast amounts of spoil from underneath the River Thames with their bare hands . . . No contest, really. They gave me a bit of a hammering and dislocated my shoulder.

At that moment, round the corner came Jack and two other rather well-built constables in the night car. Tables turned and both men were arrested and taken to the nick.

The following day the two Irishmen were given a local remand in the cells by the magistrates to appear before them again when the papers were ready. There was no delay because there was no such time-wasting organisation called the Crown Prosecution Service in those days.

On the following Friday these two appeared before a wonderful lady Chairman of Magistrates who had always regarded the Dartford policemen as HER policemen.

She listened intently to the evidence, glowering continually at the two men. I had presented my evidence with my arm still in the sling (something the inspector had instructed me to do, even though the dislocation had been satisfactorily replaced by the casualty officer and was on the mend, although still rather sore).

Both men were then jailed for three months for criminal damage and assault on a police officer occasioning actual bodily harm.

With such a penalty being fully reported in the local press, it was no surprise that the constabulary were viewed with a very healthy respect amongst the residents and visitors to Dartford. We could, with confidence, deal with everything that we were confronted by, with the assurance and knowledge that we would receive the full backing of our senior officers and the court.

The Kent Police have always been to the fore in the use of dogs to assist them, both in public order and in crime detection. The breed of dog was usually an Alsatian and the dog handlers were a dedicated group who always seemed to be working nights.

I have always had respect for the dog handlers and did, indeed, apply to join their ranks before something more appealing to me as a family man turned up.

My first experience of the skill of the dog and his handler was when we were called out to assist in a situation where a parked-up van, laden with ladders and builders tools had apparently been broken into and the ladders stolen from the roof rack.

This had occurred in the early hours of the morning and had been witnessed by an elderly lady who had heard a noise outside and seen the thief at work. She had telephoned the police station to report what she was watching.

I had responded to the call from my nearby point, and a dog handler turned up as well. The dog immediately found a good track leading from the van, through nearby alleys and pathways to the rear of a council house. We surrounded the house—all three of us—and hammered on the door.

Who was to answer it, but the owner of the van who was unaware that anything had happened since he had left the vehicle, complete with ladders, a couple of hours earlier! So we all trooped back to the van where the man confirmed that ladders and tools that had been with the van had been stolen.

The dog handler decided to cast another trail, mainly to placate the rather angry owner. After a while the dog seemed to pick up another trail and followed it to another house some 200 yards away.

We were not going to make another similar mistake so we searched the area, including the garden, where there was a ladder lying against a wall. We called the owner over and he then saw a bag, containing his tools, close to the ladder. Case solved.

The man in the house was arrested and, after the dog trail was explained to him, he admitted that he had, indeed, stolen the ladders because he wanted work as an odd job man but didn't have any equipment.

I hope that the police dog got an extra feed of biscuits that morning. It was quite an astonishing track, over dry pavements, and proved that those dogs did, indeed, have a remarkable ability.

That same dog and handler were again very successful after a high-value burglary of jewels and other effects from a large house in one of the more affluent parts of the town.

The thief had been disturbed by the owner and a police car was on the scene very quickly. No getaway car had been heard so the dog handler was called and was also on the scene very quickly.

It had been early in the morning in June and first light was already in the sky. With open fields on three sides, there was a good chance that the offender might have hidden up in the near vicinity.

The dog started a good trail straight away and headed into a copse where it barked. The handler called out that he had found some property and continued the search. This went on for several minutes, with items of the proceeds being "sniffed" by the police dog whilst still following the trail.

Finally, the dog came upon the burglar hiding in a clump of stinging nettles, in tears from the discomfort, and he was arrested. It turned out that every piece of property that had been stolen and thrown away by the thief whist trying to escape was recovered. They really are amazing animals.

CHAPTER 6

The Case of the Re-appearing Body

IT WAS DURING the summer that I found myself walking the town beat on a still and balmy night. It had been very quiet thus far and, at 3.30am, after shaking hands with every shop door handle in the shopping centre, it was almost time to make my way back to the nick for a nice cup of tea. I stood back in a doorway at the corner of High Street and Hythe Street writing in my pocketbook when I heard the sound of a vehicle coming along Hythe Street towards my position. I waited to record the number as "a vehicle seen at night" but heard it stop in the lay-by outside the General Post Office, some 50 yards to the right of my concealed doorway. I then heard two doors slam and the low sound of voices, including some laughter. Next, I heard the doors slam again and the engine re-started. I saw the headlights as the car accelerated away from the lay-by. Perhaps a letter had been posted?

As the vehicle passed my position and turned right up Lowfield Street towards Crayford, I was surprised to see that it was a police vehicle.

The unusual thing was that it was not a Kent vehicle but a Metropolitan police van with two uniformed officers, one with sergeant's stripes, sitting in the front seats. What was going on?

I left my sheltered doorway and walked back along Hythe Street towards the Post Office. As I came to the forecourt, I saw, on the steps of the entranceway to the Post Office, what seemed to be a bundle of old clothes which, I was certain, had not been there ten minutes earlier.

I went up to the steps to inspect the clothing and saw that, within the old greatcoat, was the dead body of a male.

Why had the Metropolitan Police left the body of a deceased person at the Post Office? On looking closer, the deceased was at least in his 70s and had several days' growth of beard. He appeared to be stiff with rigor mortis, indicating that death occurred at least 12 hours before—probably more. He had no teeth and his clothes were extremely filthy and shabby. His shoes were worn through. He was, fairly obviously, a dead itinerant person.

Whilst our training had always impressed upon us the need to take decisions on the merits of the situation, I felt that I should ask for the sergeant's help on this one.

I used the telephone in the adjacent public telephone box to advise the police station and spoke to the station officer. He told me that Sergeant Wills was presently taking his refreshment break, which would mean interrupting the man and risking his wrath at such an intrusion. He finally came to the phone with dire warnings of extra duties if my reason was at all frivolous, so I quickly outlined my problem to him. "Quick Sarg—dead body—Post Office—left on the steps by the Met boys", or something like that.

In his usual steady manner he agreed to come down and see me and he duly arrived in the blue van some minutes later. He also examined the body, rather more closely than I had done, and agreed that the deceased was a very dead vagrant who had been dumped on us by the Met.

This was a serious problem with serious consequences. We should give him back to them.

Clearly, they had considered that the necessary paperwork could be simply avoided by passing the problem over the police boundary into Kent.

I helped Sergeant Wills load the body into the back of the police van. Sergeant Wills then drove over the police boundary to Crayford, which was the nearest town policed by the Metropolitan Police. We unloaded the body outside the main gate of the Dog Racing Stadium and made him comfortable on the step.

Thus rid of the burden, we returned to Dartford for that well-earned cup of tea, waving cheerily at an unsuspecting passing Metropolitan squad car en route.

I still wonder what the Met officers would have offered as an explanation if I had interrupted them in the middle of their plan.

I would have had to be completely truthful as to the circumstances of my discovery which would have led, no doubt, to extreme problems for those responsible.

Moreover, I wonder what would have happened if we had been intercepted with the dead body in the back of our van.

What if I had dealt with the death as if I had come across the body in the course of my normal patrol? This is clearly what the officers from the Metropolitan Police intended.

I would have arranged for the body to be certified as dead and to be conveyed to the mortuary. A post mortem examination would be carried out as this would be an absolute requirement leading on from the circumstances of such a sudden death.

There would have to be an Inquest. The Coroner would have asked me to explain the circumstances of how the discovery had been made.

Here was a body displaying the effects of rigor mortis on the steps of the town's post office where, if death had occurred at least 12 hours earlier, as indicated by the degree of rigor mortis, customers would have been stepping over him.

Why had I not found the body when I first patrolled this street earlier in my period of duty?

Surely, I would have to be truthful and describe the circumstances as I witnessed them. Such an explanation would be, at the very least, embarrassing for the officers responsible—possibly career-ending.

I also wonder whatever happened to the poor soul who had to undergo all those unwarranted journeys.

CHAPTER 7

Dealing with Road Traffic

DARTFORD IS LOCATED along the main route between Dover and London. Historically it was a stopping point for the Romans 2000 years ago who built Watling Street between London and Dover. There was a ford over the River Darenth, with an associated settlement at that point. In the fifth century, West Kent, including the Dartford area, was settled by Saxon tribes and Frankish people from Germany, Northern France and Belgium. Entries in the Domesday Book compiled by the Normans in 1086 demonstrate that the Saxon settlements, which evolved over a period of five hundred years or more, were well administered and organised, with an emphasis on agriculture. Chaucer's Pilgrims passed through the town on their journey to Canterbury. Wat Tyler and his men were thought to have taken victuals in the town on their way to meeting up with other countrymen at Blackheath for the Peasants' Revolt in 1381 and there is a public house in the High Street named after him. Samuel Pepys probably stopped his horse at the Bull & George hostelry in the 17th century and took refreshment when making his journeys to Chatham Dockyard in connection with his duties concerning the Naval Fleet of King Charles II. Dickens also must have been a frequent traveller through the town in the 19th century as many of his tales are sourced in north Kent.

Dartford is, therefore, a place of great history which became an ancient coaching town on the major east-west route between the English Channel, Dover, Canterbury, Rochester and London.

There are many establishments still in existence in the town centre which are dedicated to the traveller but, because of its narrow streets and hilly approaches from either direction, the twentieth-century motorised traffic bottlenecked the old town centre.

In the 1950s and 1960s a police-manned traffic point was operated between 8am and 6pm each weekday to control traffic flow in the centre of the town where High Street met Lowfield Street. Police Officers, equipped with white armlets, or, when wet, full length white rubberised coats, were engaged in the manual direction of traffic.

For periods of about one hour duration, the officer would be acting as a human windmill, directing the cars, vans, lorries and buses in a hoped-for continuous flow. Sergeant Sellars would have been proud of the results of the training he had given to his charges at Sandgate. The close proximity of passing vehicles often caused concern, with the wheels of double-decker buses passing over the top of a toecap of one's smart duty boot being a frequent event.

Every morning and evening heavy local traffic brought the town centre to a standstill, notwithstanding the efforts of the uniformed windmills. Most of the drivers using the town centre, particularly at the rush hour, were local and well used to the antics of the policeman on duty. They readily responded to the flick of a finger or glance of the head to accept their turn to move forward. A smile or nod passed between them always helped the atmosphere.

A congested town centre was probably the reason why, in the first half of the 20th century, the main arterial road known as the A2 was built for the fast modern car and commercial lorry to bypass the town to the south.

This road, in the 1960s, was a very fast three-lane, single-carriage highway, since superseded even further to the south by the much newer motorway-standard dual carriageway, linking up with the orbital M25 circling London.

The old arterial A2, known as Princes Road, had one lane east, one lane west, with a suicide lane running up the middle of the road for those drivers who wished to risk their lives in overtaking the slower moving lorries and cars.

For a multiplicity of reasons, many drivers failed to appreciate the danger of oncoming cars sharing this centre lane, with many more foolishly believing that they could pass just one more car before moving back to the safety of the nearside lane. Misjudgement of speed and distance by some drivers meant that the frequency of head-on collisions was frightening.

Hardly a week went by without a very serious, or even fatal, accident occurring during the daily rush to or from London. When the inevitable call was received, the entire section scrambled to get to the scene in company with the ambulance and, frequently, the fire brigade.

Cars built in that era were not designed to crumple and collapse; they just bent or exploded into a fireball, sometimes causing the most horrific injuries. Without seatbelts, head injuries and chest injuries were most common.

Exiting the front of the car from the passenger seat by way of the broken windscreen was a fairly common means of leaving the car, albeit without choice.

Within my first year at Dartford I was a seasoned and somewhat cynical provider of care to victims, having seen and dealt with several deceased drivers and passengers. I was well accustomed to arriving at the scene of a bloody consequence of some driver's foolish actions to see the gathered crowd of onlookers move back with the comment. "Oh, it's all right now. Here come the police." (Sergeant Mallard was proved accurate in his farewell advices to us from training school!) Strewth! I wasn't yet 20 years of age, and they expected me to be able to deal professionally and swiftly with the incident so that their journey could be continued as promptly as possible.

One of the most-asked questions by other motorists at a head-on collision blocking the A2 was "How long before we can get past? We've been here twenty minutes already".

If I had had a crystal ball, I could have advised them to come back in 40 years to see how long the police, fire brigade, highways agency, *et al*, take to clear a scene these days. They shut the road all day now and call it a crime scene, causing delay and inconvenience to thousands of road users who deserve to be allowed to continue their journey without the ridiculous delays frequently enforced upon them by what is loosely called "the emergency services".

One of the worst accidents I experienced on the A2 was shortly after I received a driving permit and was attempting to stop and check what turned out to be a stolen Vauxhall Velox car with two young male occupants.

It was a very wet and dark February evening with light drizzle falling and we had been travelling across Dartford Heath towards London. At that time, there were no street lights or other residual areas of light to illuminate the area. Without headlamps, the surrounding area was totally black. Heavy traffic was still leaving the city of London.

It appeared that as soon as the Vauxhall driver realised that a police van was behind him, he increased his speed to try and get away and pulled out into the "suicide" lane in the centre of the carriageway to pass a flat-nosed yellow Bedford Dormobile.

This manoeuvre was in total disregard for the presence of the headlamps of an approaching saloon car which was already occupying the centre lane. Amazingly, the approaching car had just passed a blue Bedford Dormobile of the same model as the west-bound Bedford. Neither car in the centre lane had time to return to their respective inside lanes and they collided head-on.

The side of the Vauxhall spun left and hit the blue Dormobile which careered across the road and hit the yellow Dormobile head-on. The impacts were substantial and two young ladies who had been sitting in armchairs in the back of the yellow van were catapulted forward, through both windscreens and ended up in the back of the blue van. They were both in their 20s and one had been a beauty queen.

I stopped my police car in the middle of the carnage and shouted for help on the radio.

To get out of a police car as first officer at the scene, armed only with a basic first-aid kit, is a very sobering experience. The Stygian scene had become totally dark and silent, other than for the moaning of the injured. No training fully prepares an officer for such a sudden rush of priorities. My heart still goes out to anyone who is faced with the aftermath of sudden tragedy, be it a road accident, train crash or bomb.

Where does one start? I did manage to recall one priority. That was to put the urgent request in for help on the police radio. I then arranged for useful people to be allocated suitable jobs.

Immediate attention was given to First aid. Traffic control and the consideration for motorists caught up in the confusion were not immediately considered.

I was lucky to have been in a good radio reception area and my call to Operations Room for support was immediately acknowledged and I was assured that lots of help was on its way. I had called for four ambulances and the Fire Brigade and they were all needed.

Almost at once, help was volunteered from members of the public who had been forced to a halt because of the wreckage across the road. One well-dressed middle-aged man came to me and said, "I am a dentist. Can I help?" I directed him to one of the young ladies who was obviously suffering from severe facial injury and said, "She seems to have lost a lot of teeth. What can you do for her?"

The next ten to fifteen minutes spent in expectation of assistance seemed like hours. I directed other helpful civilians to tend to the injured and tried my best to stop arterial bleeding from one of the drivers whose steering wheel had broken into his chest and neck. Finally, through my own haze, I recognised that major help had arrived and the injured were taken away to various local hospitals.

Wreckage was moved and traffic was released past the scene by my colleagues. I went and sat down on the kerb and got out my cigarettes and realised that my whole body was trembling.

It was just then that the duty inspector arrived and came up to me. Seeing that I was sitting on the verge having a cigarette whilst everyone else was going in all directions, he shouted at me for my idleness. I have to admit that I was not exactly polite in response but when he realised what my involvement had been, he instructed another officer to be the Reporting Officer, allowing me to be a witness.

The consequence of this accident was that nine persons were taken to hospital with eight of them suffering from severe head injuries.

Both girls had suffered horrendous facial lacerations and broken jaws. Four of the injured went straight into intensive care but all eventually recovered, although very badly scarred.

The driver of the Vauxhall car was committed to the Crown Court at Canterbury several months later where he was convicted of taking and driving away a motor car, but the jury found him not guilty of dangerous driving because not one other member of the public was able to recall what happened, so badly affected had they been by the trauma. It was my word against the two young men and the jury chose to believe the car thieves over my account.

Even in those days the Crown could not afford to pay for good prosecution barristers, whilst the defendants and their insurance companies were able to pay for the best defences.

It was to be several years afterwards that the police trained their traffic division officers in the art of Accident Investigation whereby expert evidence could be presented to the courts to corroborate witnesses statements and give credibility to the facts.

It was whilst building upon my experience of dealing with such tragic events that I, like many mature emergency workers, became hardened to the sight and sound of personal grief. Police station mess rooms are rarely quiet and contemplative after such serious incidents. Some wit would always try and release the tension with black humour or a topical quip.

Neither the general public nor the politicians who make laws regarding political correctness would fully appreciate the relief that the release of humour brings to the aftermath of such shock.

Following a particularly nasty head-on collision on the main A2 road between a lorry and an inebriated motorcyclist late one night, the ambulance crew notified the duty officer at the scene that they appeared to have a body with only one leg. It became obvious that it had not been a one-legged rider who was now deceased, and we were now going to have to search for the missing limb.

The scene was exceedingly dark and police lighting consisted of a couple of low-powered torches with which we set-to and combed the undergrowth and bushes close to the scene. It actually took nearly an hour and extra lighting from traffic division to find the leg some ten feet up in the branches of a hawthorn bush some 30 yards from the impact point.

Boy! Had he been travelling! Comments such as "Legless both before and after impact" do actually take away the tension of dealing with nasty incidents.

The people I found to have the driest senses of humour were frequently men involved in the medical field—ambulance men, doctors, morticians. Their sometimes ghoulish humour is probably presented as a barrier between the associated miseries connected to their job and their desire to keep sane.

Stress management and counselling were two areas that had not yet been recognised, so one just joked about the event, in private, and got on with life.

Whilst the modern emergency services are equipped with fast cars and excellent equipment to enable them to deal with their urgent situation, it was not always so.

As a sub-divisional motorcyclist, I was the dogs-body who was usually sitting in the police station catching up on weeks of backlogged work. This made my position self-perpetuating because should an emergency call be received, and no-one in that area was detailed to be standing by a telephone box making a point at that moment, it came down to a choice of one as to whom should attend.

On with the old Corker crash helmet, mount up the Velocette LI 150, switch on the headlamp and dash off to the incident at speeds sometimes approaching 25 miles-per-hour.

One cold, rainy day, a call came in regarding an accident that had occurred at Six Wents, a major junction on the A2 to the east of the town.

This route would take me up the long rise of Princes Road from Lowfield Street traffic junction towards Gravesend.

I joined the traffic, switched on the headlight of my old Velocette and coaxed the maximum speed out of the clapped-out, water-cooled engine. I moved out into the centre lane to pass a large lorry laden with rolls of paper from Bowater's Paper Works but my speed was only marginally faster than that of the old Foden truck.

Working my way along his offside length I reached the point beside the driver's cab when my motorcycle became adversely affected by the dam of air being forced around the flat front of the lorry.

There was no way that my motorcycle's wide fairing and lack of horsepower could overcome this air dam and I looked up to the driver's window for help. He opened his window and looked down at me as if I shouldn't be there.

"Excuse me, driver", I shouted, "Could you just slow down a little bit so that I can get past. I am on an emergency call to an accident up ahead."

"OK, mate," he replied.

He took his foot from the accelerator and I was able to break the air dam and pass the lorry, arriving at the scene a minute or so later.

At no time was that aged Velocette able to reach even 40 miles-per-hour.

I have already mentioned the construction of the Dartford Tunnel that was due for completion in the mid 1960s. This also meant major roadworks to join up the main roads through our area with the tunnel approaches.

Underway at one of the major junctions of the A2 was the building of a huge roundabout on Princes Road, where the A2 was to pass over the top of the newly constructed tunnel approach, now the M25, South Orbital motorway.

The roundabout construction had resulted in a great many cones and signs being placed on the approaches to the construction scene, which was all within an established 40mph area.

At 2am one morning, we had a call to a spectacular single-vehicle accident at the roundabout.

On attendance, we found that a Humber Super Snipe Estate car, which was one of the most powerful estates made around that time, had been travelling towards London along Princes Road and, for some reason, the driver had not recognised the plethora of signs and cones designed to bring attention to drivers that they were about to reach an area where caution would be needed. The tyre skid marks became visible some 200 yards before the metal barrier surrounding the actual roundabout, beyond which was a drop down onto the tunnel approach road that ran beneath the A2 and still, as yet, unmade.

The car had skidded out of control for over 200 yards, taken out a couple of directional signs, demolished the new steel Armco barrier which was supported by 10inch oak posts driven into the ground, taken off, and nose-dived into the ground forty feet below. Witnesses variously estimated his speed at between 100 and 120 miles-per-hour, a fact seemingly confirmed by the wreckage, tyre marks and damaged Armco.

It took the fire brigade nearly an hour to release the driver, who was a young car thief, from the vehicle which was virtually unrecognisable as a Humber. Someone had to tell his parents . . .

For those readers who are familiar with it, one of the largest out-of-town shopping centres in Europe is Bluewater, just a couple of miles to the east of Dartford, accessed from the A2 road.

In the 1960s, the site was a disused chalk quarry, long since abandoned and having a large lake formed at its base—hence the name of Bluewater.

Most people, whilst driving along the A2 towards Rochester, or London, were totally unaware of its presence because of the wide grass verge, strong fence and thick hedgerow on the northern side of the road.

Immediately beyond the fence and hedgerow was a drop of some 150-200 feet to the base of the quarry. The first ten feet or so was almost sheer, down to a ledge some ten feet wide. The sheer drop then fell away from that ledge to the bottom.

Dartford officers knew of this dangerous area from their local knowledge.

So it was that when a call was received from a motorist who had witnessed a car leave the road on the north side and disappear through the hedge, we all thought the worst.

Cars attended at the scene and the skid marks were found that showed the car had lost control and slid over the grass and through the hedge, leaving a large hole. There was a gap in the bushes and, beyond that, fresh air! No car.

We ventured to the edge of the quarry and looked over, just in time to see a young man scrambling to reach the top of the quarry. We pulled him up and saw that, apart from minor injuries, he was fit enough. We then shone our lights down and there, upside down on the ten-foot wide ledge, was what turned out to be a Morris Mini.

The young man said that his girlfriend was still in the car so we climbed down, using some long branches as aids. We were able to get the young lady out of the car and up to the grass verge. She was also only slightly injured but relieved to be back up on the road level.

Then somebody said to the couple that they were very lucky not to have gone all the way down. It was only then did they realise that their car had stopped on the ledge and if they had got out the wrong side, it was a 200ft sheer drop into the darkness beyond and they were dead.

The poor girl fainted and ended up in a worse condition than she had been when the car came to rest.

As the sub-divisional motorcyclist I was always moaning about the lack of speed available from the water-cooled Velocette. In time, one of these ancient hand gear-change motorbikes was replaced by a smart new Ariel Leader 250cc two-stroke motorcycle. This was able to reach speeds of up to seventy miles-per-hour, but the downside was the smoke.

Although two-stroke fuel was available to be dispensed at garage filling stations, the police were equipped with a police station petrol pump and its own storage tanks.

In order that the petrol could be converted into two-stroke fuel, a couple of shots of oil had to be added to each gallon of the petrol.

The oil supplied for police vehicle use was called KCC6, which loosely stood for "the oil that the Kent County Council reclaimed from its drains and re-cycled for use over and over again".

It wasn't exactly as viscous and perfect as that provided in bottles by the likes of Esso or BP. In fact, Domestos might have been a good alternative.

On a still day, the route taken by the Ariel Leader to an incident could be followed for the next hour by any other attendees, merely by following the plumes of white oil smoke which hung low over the road.

There was the time that the Mayor of Dartford was hosting a visit from a minor Royal personage and I had been selected to be the motorcycle escort to clear the route through the town centre.

Because it is usual for official cavalcades to travel sedately through areas of sightseers, I led the line of official vehicles down into the town at a slow speed so that the appropriate waving could be carried out by both celebrity and crowd alike.

On reaching the traffic point in the town centre, I found that the officer on point duty was unaware of our approach and I was forced to come to a halt at the tail of queuing traffic.

When the traffic moved forward again and I selected first gear to do likewise, the engine stalled. This was probably because it had gummed up through not being revved fast enough during the slow drive along the route.

I hastily kick-started the machine and fiercely revved up a couple of times so as to clear the cylinders of the soot and waste matter that had accumulated in the cylinders and then moved off.

I glanced behind me to check on the motorcade and couldn't see it anywhere. All I could see was a cloud of thick white smoke filling the entire width of Hythe Street between the tall shop buildings on either side of the road. Those persons not in the smoke laden area were laughing, whilst I expect those within the dense oil-laden fog were coughing.

I did not hang around at the end of the route for the usual thanks from the mayor, and the Ariel was not used for escort duty again.

CHAPTER 8

Public Order

THERE ALWAYS HAVE been, and will always be, public order problems in towns and urban areas such as Dartford. Many unruly children will inevitably progress into disobedient and disrespectful youths. A percentage of those will in turn become lawbreakers and some of those will, without doubt, become recidivists. Unfortunately, countless families will have had generations of experiencing conflict with police officers. To some, it is an inevitable way of life, the secret of which, I think, may lie in their genes. Successive governments, councils and other official bodies spend time and money in attempting to create a respectful and law-abiding resolution to these families' lives but it will be doomed to continued failure because of the entrenched attitude that these families hold against a civil life.

Dartford had the usual listing of troublesome families, with their teenage offspring frequently testing the patience of authority, especially when they had been experiencing the joys of imbibing alcohol and drugs.

We had our fair share of broken windows, noisy fights and other associated stupid town-centre behaviour but the police in Dartford seemed to be held in general respect by most citizens with the result that "policing by consent" was still a valid maxim.

A quiet word with a miscreant, possibly in an alley or other quiet place away from his mates, would usually do the trick.

Being a copper used to be regarded as 20 per cent law and 80per cent psychology. I fear that the formula has been more than turned upside down in the 21st century.

The present *de rigueur* use of body armour and riot helmets had also not yet been considered. Indeed, it would be at least another ten years before the emergency use of residential dustbin lids or even entire empty dustbins, at times of public disorder, was abandoned. Senior Officers realised, at last, that better protection would have to be provided and we started to see officers using polycarbonate shields for the upper body, cricket boxes for the genital area and football shin-guards for the legs.

It is, perhaps, fortunate that helmets and body protection are now supplied as a matter of course because, with the demise of the old metal dustbin, the thought of wearing a black plastic wheelie bin as a body shield might be considered rather silly.

Inter-town enmity between the youngsters was evident in most towns like Dartford and probably started in the school playground with silly gangs having arguments over territory.

On Tuesday evenings there was rarely any problem in Dartford town centre. This was because the Dartford boys used to travel in the London Transport number 96 bus, or by scooter and motorcycle, to Bexleyheath to beat up the Bexleyheath boys.

However, on Thursdays the late-turn police stayed on after 10pm to assist the night duty because the Bexleyheath boys could be expected to make their return visit to Dartford to make their own demonstration of intended power and control.

This routine seemed to be an established "Rite of Passage" for any working class (and some better bred) teenager from the London suburbs and associated districts.

Whitsun Bank Holiday weekend in 1964 was a particularly busy time. We were aware from news reports that the mods and rockers had decided to pay a visit to the coastal towns in the south-east of England.

Mods were a movement of passing teenage fashion and they were formed around the start of the 1960s.

They were mainly younger people who had a shared interest in reasonably smart dress, modern music and a love of Lambretta and Vespa motor scooters which were adorned with countless wing mirrors and aerials. Their choice of outer garment was the brown or khaki parka under which was reasonably smart attire.

The rockers on the other hand, were a less tidy group of youngsters who enjoyed heavy rock music, noisy motorcycles and leather. They wanted to emulate the "Hell's Angels" sects that were sweeping America at the time.

Like oil and water, their interests clashed to the point of violence and visits to coastal resorts on Bank Holidays gave the opportunity for these two groups to interact, with the result that the police had to intervene to restore order.

My home town of Margate was a particular venue for their own choice of amusement. Clacton and Southend in Essex, and Brighton in West Sussex also experienced problems but Margate almost had a full-blown riot on its hands.

On that Whitsun Bank Holiday Monday I had been asleep at my lodgings, when, at 5am, I was awoken by one of the night duty officers.

He told me to be ready in full uniform in thirty minutes, complete with a box of sandwiches, when I would be collected by the police van. I was going to spend the day at the seaside but wouldn't need a bucket and spade.

At 9.00am that day, on arrival at the coast, we pulled up in a line of miscellaneous police transport on the approach to Margate railway station. Probably 100 police officers were standing around waiting for instructions.

Milling round the seafront area were scores of parka-clad youths and, further along the road, and on the beach, were groups of leather-clad individuals. By the state of many of them, they had spent the night sleeping rough on the beach or in nearby parkland. The mods and rockers were in Margate town but it was still peaceful—Just.

It wasn't long before things warmed up and the confrontations became more interesting.

At one point about twenty mods jumped down from the promenade onto Marine Sands and started to smash up some deckchairs. They wielded the broken pieces of deckchair and charged down towards a group of rockers who had been at the waters edge, minding their own business.

This aggression led to an even larger group of rockers joining the fray and, in a minute or so, we found ourselves in amongst the mayhem doing the same thing as the two other factions.

We managed to pinpoint the leaders who were duly arrested and dragged away. Without leaders, the fighting died again.

Squads of police officers from all over Kent were instructed to patrol the Golden Mile and prevent the two sides from becoming over-excited but, as the day wore on, more youths arrived on their various means of transport and, by lunchtime, Margate Police Station had a queue of arresting officers, together with their captives, waiting to be processed by the overworked station officers.

Many fights had broken out over the course of the morning and early afternoon between the two factions, both on the seafront and on the beach. Most were fisticuff skirmishes but some involved weapons.

There were some injuries but perhaps not enough for the photographers and press, whose appetite for trouble can never be satisfied.

Some journalists and photographers who were present to record this Bank Holiday mayhem were actively encouraging some youths to show off so that there would be good copy for the newspapers the following day.

Holidaying families either went home early or stood around watching, as if at some organised sports event.

We later found out that there had been plans in the early afternoon for the Mayor of Margate to read the Riot Act. This would have meant a totally different situation, with the police having powers to arrest everyone who remained in the area.

It was true that at one point, officers were told to draw truncheons and to charge a large group of deckchair-hurling miscreants, whose behaviour was extremely threatening to members of the general public. We went willingly into the melee but only a few arrests were made for being involved in the general disorder.

Most of the troublemakers immediately dissolved into ineffective smaller groups. The bare-faced challenges to police authority, as seen in recent city disturbances, simply just did not happen in those days of an effective police force.

For the officers from locations such as Dartford, Gravesend and Chatham, who were used to town-centre public order breakdown, there was a general attitude of gung ho. Diving into an area of fighting teenagers whilst having confidence in your uniform, seemed to have the desired effect, especially as a great number of youths in one particular area were our own local troublemakers from Dartford and the surrounding area.

We recognised them and they, with a degree of resignation, recognised us. The words, "I know where you live. I'll tell your mother." were heard to be uttered before some degree of untidy departure from the town took place.

The Riot Act remained unread that day and, for that, many breathed a huge sigh of relief.

We were finally released to return to our home towns in the late evening but were obliged to deviate to isolated skirmishes that broke out, mainly in the pubs adjacent to the A2 throughout the north Kent towns.

Some people just did not know when to stop.

CHAPTER 9

Caravan Dwellers and Gypsies

IN 1964 THE London borough of Bromley took steps to evict a large community of caravan dwellers who had been living illegally in the south-east London area. The consequence of this eviction led to about 20 caravans and their occupants setting up camp between the villages of Stone and Bean, a couple of miles to the east of Dartford. This illegal encampment was positioned on both sides of the main arterial road between London and Dover known as the A2 where there were wide grass verges. The Kent County Council, which was ultimately responsible for the verges of this highway, took no immediate action and within a few months there were well over 100 caravans, together with a motley collection of assorted pick-up trucks, vans, and cars, not to mention horses and dogs. Long lines of washing were strung along the fences and hedgerows, with children as young as two regularly sitting on the kerbstones throwing sticks and other objects at passing traffic. Great piles of scrap metal and old furniture built up along the previously pristine verges. Clearly something had to be done. The local council seemed powerless and so it came down to the police to act.

By parking their caravans on the public highway, it was deemed that they were committing an act of wilful obstruction as laid down in statute law by s.121 Highways Act 1959, and could be summoned for that offence.

It was necessary to establish some degree of polite dialogue with the itinerant people and this was achieved by the use of common sense and a friendly approach. After all, we preferred to have such people on our side rather against us when they outnumbered the policemen on duty at any time by 20 to 1! Next—Step forward the sub-divisional motor cyclist.

For several months, along with other officers, my weekly duties included regular dealings with the families and I got to know them quite well. They gave many explanations for their behaviour, mostly untrue, but they responded to fair treatment.

On Monday, I rode out to their location, arriving before the menfolk left on their daily routines of totting and dealing. I then walked both lengths of the north and south verges, taking sufficient details for identification. As appropriate, they were reported for obstruction or offences of encamping on the highway.

On Tuesday, I submitted the process cards and they were hurried through the necessary administration into the court box.

On Wednesday, summonses were applied for.

On Thursday, I went back to the site to serve the summonses.

Friday was the day that they were summoned to appear, which filled the court by 9.30am. They were then swiftly wheeled in front of the magistrate and each received a £1 fine which was paid to the Clerk of the Court without delay.

They treated it like a weekly rent and considered it a good result if other police work took priority and we couldn't get around to the site on a Monday.

And they say that the wheels of justice grind slowly. Not with the caravan dwellers, it didn't.

It was very many months before the caravan dwellers finally left the verges and they probably returned back to Orpington, from whence they had come in the first place.

We had cause to be thankful for the considerable strength of one particular itinerant. There had been a head-on collision fairly close to the encampment and one of the drivers was trapped in his car because, amongst other severe damage, the "A" frame had collapsed on him.

The man was losing blood at a fast rate but the fire brigade had to come from Gravesend.

We did not have the tools, or the strength, to extract the man from the collapsed frame that was encapsulating him in the twisted metal of his wreckage.

Enter Big Wally. Wally Smith was one of the caravan dwellers who, with his family, had taken up residence on the grass verge some months earlier.

The area round his caravan was always a mass of old cookers, angle iron and other detritus from the various sources of acquisition that he frequented in his course of business.

He was a giant of a man, well over six-feet-six-inches, who tossed scrap iron as easily as wedding guests threw confetti. We were very concerned about the state of the injured man.

There were about five police officers and two ambulance crews trying their best to prevent blood loss from the victim, and attempting all sorts of ideas to try and release him when Wally arrived at his caravan in his tax-less, insurance-less, pick-up truck and hauled his huge body from the cab.

He could see our problem and came over to ask if he could help. I already knew him well from the Monday morning visits and he was, at least, respectful towards me. I asked him if he had any long pieces of iron with which we could lever the door frame open to release the man.

Wally rolled up his sleeves and demonstrated his enormous strength by putting one foot against the "A" frame and pulling back on the door frame. There was a grinding of metal as his mighty efforts widened the driver's door area thereby facilitating our effective and safe removal of the driver.

First aid was given and he later recovered from his injuries.

After the accident had finally been cleared, and traffic was moving normally again, we were invited into Wally's caravan for a cup of tea, made by his very ample wife. This incident gave a chance for us to further improve our relationship with the caravan dwellers which led to a lot less tension being experienced between the police and the local gypsies.

I managed to get Wally mentioned in the local newspaper and read it to him and his wife when I next went to the caravan, his skills not extending to the ability to read newsprint. He was very happy indeed and I left on the very best of terms with the big man.

From time to time, many members of the gypsy fraternity were involved in conflict with the police, frequently in the late evening after a drinking session.

Some of the younger members brought themselves to notice by engaging in crime or criminal damage, making police intervention necessary, frequently leading to prosecution.

Maintaining an understanding and degree of respect with the likes of Wally was a very important part of police work, given that we had very little manpower in those days. At least he could bang heads together in order that the young tearaways received some understanding of growing up a touch more sensibly than if they were simply allowed to run riot like many of them do today.

An incident with a gypsy from the Bexley area proved that, when alcohol had been taken to excess, the ability to feel pain is substantially reduced.

A call was received from a night watchman in a run-down factory area of the town during the early hours, which resulted in the entire town night-duty racing to the scene in two cars and one push-bike.

Our informant had heard a crash within an adjoining property and suspected people breaking into the premises.

The five of us surrounded the area and started searching.

I climbed up onto a wall and looked over the corrugated asbestos roof to see a hole in the centre. This roofing material was rather brittle and was not designed to be climbed on without the use of a ladder or duckboards to spread the load.

The shattered asbestos sheeting was entirely consistent with somebody having fallen through the flat roof, probably whilst trying to break in. There is little other reason for someone to want to trespass in such a way without some greater criminal intent.

I could also hear the sound of what I thought was heavy breathing coming from below the hole. There was no way I was going to climb across the roof, so I told the senior constable what I had had seen and heard.

There was definitely someone inside so we leant against the door until it became insecure—it took three of us to achieve this—and we entered the light industrial lock-up. There, under the hole in the roof was one of our traveller friends who was asleep, or unconscious, on the floor, with a pool of blood underneath him. His snoring proved that he was still alive.

After some minutes we were able to rouse him from what was a drunken stupor and he started complaining that his head and arm hurt but seemed to accept our accomplishment in finding him as inevitable.

He was taken back to the car and we could see by the headlamps that his right arm was severely lacerated leading to a substantial blood loss. We bound it up with a dressing from the first aid kit and took him back to Dartford Police Station where the sergeant was apprised of the arrest.

By this time, the offender, John Smith (they were all called John Smith) was complaining that his arm was cut, but he didn't know how this had occurred. The sergeant undid the bandage we had wrapped round the arm and saw the extent of the jagged slice of flesh that was hanging from the lower arm. "That will have to be cleaned up before you go to hospital," said the sergeant.

He then took him to the sink in the cell passage and commenced to clean the wound with a scrubbing brush and scouring powder.

So inebriated was the gypsy that only a mild complaint of pain was received whilst the dirt and asbestos splinters were cleared from the flesh.

Thus sanitized and re-bandaged, we took Smith to the West Hill general hospital where the casualty officer, before stitching the arm with some 30 sutures, commented in glowing terms as to the way that the wound had been cleaned.

Following a sleep in the cells, Smith later told the CID that he was taking a short cut home from the pub and that somebody pushed him into a hole. Any recollection of climbing onto the roof of business premises with intent to steal, and crashing through the roof in the attempt, was totally absent from his memory.

In another case there was a character with gypsy blood who was a regular visitor to the town centre and known as Tom.

He dealt in scrap metal and involved himself in what is known as general dealing, meaning he handled anything if it was worth his while. Now Tom liked his pint as well as the next man but it did go to his head after a few, resulting in his long conviction list for assault and similar offences when drunk.

One night, it was said that he had been drinking on his own when he got into a bit of a fisticuffs with another local ne'er-do-well. The landlord ejected them both and they continued their argument outside.

What happened next is unclear but the partner of the ne'er-do-well reported the man missing the next day.

The eventual enquiries led the local CID to question Tom but he could not be charged with anything through lack of evidence.

Now Tom owned and drove (when sober) an old Vauxhall car of many years vintage and it was several weeks later when a traffic car pulled Tom over in a routine stop and asked the usual questions.

At this time, the officer noticed a bad smell and, to cut a long story short, Tom was charged with manslaughter and served a couple of years in prison for being involved in the ne'er-do-well's death, and for carrying said chap around in his boot for six weeks—in summer.

It seems that Tom was going to dump the body off somewhere but didn't actually get around to it as he couldn't find a suitable place where it wouldn't be found.

CHAPTER 10

Private Life

WELL BEFORE I had considered the possibility of becoming a police officer, I had met the girl who was to become my wife and mother of our two lovely daughters. We had become friends in 1959 and decided to become engaged in 1962, just before I left home and moved to my posting at Dartford. The plan was to be married after I had completed my two year period of probation in the force. We had, of course, hoped that my first posting would be closer to our home at Margate so that our relationship would continue relatively unchanged but things are never that straightforward and going to Dartford for the start of 1963 meant that we were apart for weeks at a time. Somehow, that relationship remained intact and we were married in September 1964.

So it was that we moved into an unfurnished ground floor flat just round the corner from Dartford Police Station. All our meagre savings had been spent on the essentials of living, with instructions given to the suppliers of furniture, carpets, domestic appliances and essential services to co-ordinate their deliveries for our day of arrival following our honeymoon.

Things never change. It wasn't until late in the evening of that first day that we even had a bed to sleep on and it was still several days later before our flat was sufficiently furnished and equipped to start an almost normal married life. My small annual leave allocation was all used up, so I was back at work straight away, leaving my wife to organise our new home.

This flat was in Priory Hill, an area of old, dilapidated terraced houses, many of which were owned by dodgy landlords, and home to many immigrant families from Asia.

Next door to us lived numerous members of the Indian sub-continent, mostly Sikhs, none of whom were familiar as permanent occupants as they went in and out in great numbers all day long, carrying their bed rolls. We never seemed to see the same person twice.

The smell of curry was all-pervasive and seemed to impregnate everything in our flat.

My colleagues often asked me how I could afford to visit the Indian Restaurant so frequently.

More than once, we were disturbed at night by the gurgling of drains, followed by the stench of sewerage emanating from the manhole cover located outside our bedroom.

Our ground-floor bedroom had old French doors opening onto a small rear yard from which the unkempt back garden rose to the rear garden wall. In this small yard area was a shared sewer drain cover. The doors formed a poor seal with the threshold of the door frame with the result that the gap allowed the sewerage that was forcing up the inspection cover to overflow into the back yard then seep into the bedroom under the door.

I still shudder at the times when I found myself in that backyard, in complete darkness, trying to build a dam of newspaper and earth in vain efforts to prevent the ingress of the vile stuff that was overflowing from the manhole.

As the house was on a hill, the contents from all the residents' sewerage pipes above us flowed down to the curry blockage of our Indian neighbours below us.

This was surely a flat that both my wife and I were anxious to move from as soon as we could afford it.

New police houses were just not being built and when existing ones became available, they were usually reserved for officers with families—not to newly-married junior officers.

It was fortuitous that, at the end of 1964, Kent Police embarked upon a programme of new homes for their officers.

This was generally taken to mean that the older, more experienced family policemen would be allocated the new houses, allowing older houses to be issued to the likes of me, and giving me the opportunity of leaving the awful rented flat. I did not think that we would qualify for one of the new homes but we were lucky.

In 1965 we moved into a brand new three-bedroom detached house in the village of Bean, some three miles from Dartford. All I had to do now was to earn enough money to put some furniture between the empty walls and some carpet on the bare floors.

Kent Police had purchased nine newly-built houses for the use of local police officers and their families. They were located on a modern residential estate and many new friends were made.

One of my Dartford colleagues, Brian, was one of our neighbours. Although he joined the force after me, he was in his late 20s with a wife and three young children.

He also owned a brand new, top of the range, maroon Ford Zephyr Zodiac which was the envy of everyone in the road. He used to give me a lift to and from work because we were on the same shift, and the comfort of such a car led to some pangs of envy on my part. All I could afford was a Vespa 150cc motor scooter.

I once asked him how he could afford such a large, modern vehicle. He told me that he had given up a job in the printing trade to join the police.

He had owned his own house in the Medway Towns and was told that he had to sell his house because his posting would be to Dartford—too far away in those days to travel daily.

At that time a police officer was not allowed to have alternative income; therefore Brian found that because he wasn't in a position to rent out his old home, he would sell it.

With the proceeds of this house sale, he made investments and bought the new car. His attitude was that, after a few years, he would be in a position to buy again, and he might as well enjoy the proceeds whilst he could.

Then came the occasion of the annual "House Inspection".

This was the day when a senior officer called to inspect the house and make sure that we hadn't chopped up the staircase for firewood, or caused other heinous damage to police property.

This time it was the Chief Superintendent of "C" Division who was to carry out the duties.

This particular chief superintendent had just taken delivery of a nice new Morris Oxford, for which he was in receipt of a mileage allowance to allow him to show it off to all and sundry.

He turned up at Brian's house and was welcomed by Brian and his wife. During conversation the Chief pointed to the Ford which was parked on the driveway, and said to Brian, "Who does the car belong to?"

Brian said, "That is mine, sir".

After receiving confirmation that he had heard correctly, it seems that the chief superintendent flew into a rage and ordered Brian to get rid of it because he was not allowed to drive such an expensive car. It was bad for the morale of other officers and was a bad advert for policemen in their endeavours to get better pay. Such was the relationship between ranks then.

Brian simply ignored the instruction and kept the car.

Early life at Bean, before I bought a car, was good although my wife would have enjoyed a touch more excitement in her day to day entertainment.

Without family transport, there was little chance for her to get out of the village. There was a small village shop and a fruit & vegetable lorry visited the estate once a week. The milkman, butcher, and baker also delivered to the door.

Those businesses provided the essential food for us, together with the very occasional journey into Dartford on the bus for extra shopping as could be afforded.

There was never much money left over at the end of the month, so trips to the cinema were rare, and entering the local public house for a pint of beer was confined to birthdays and other anniversaries.

In September 1965 we celebrated the arrival of our first daughter. I had passed my driving test and bought my first car for £105 from a neighbour across the road.

It was a 1955 Standard 8 saloon that was to carry us at speeds as high as 55 miles-per-hour around the cement-dust covered countryside of North Kent for the next year or so.

The car was to give us so much more freedom from the confines of the village. We were able to plan visits to our respective parents who lived over 50 miles away on the Kent coast.

We could also make visits to London, which was less than 20 miles from where we now lived.

CHAPTER 11

Serious Crime

HAVING NOW BEEN at Dartford for nearly three years, I frequently found myself one of the senior shift members, such was the turnover of police officers through transfer and resignation. The senior constables who had so patiently provided advice and cover for me in 1963 had mostly all retired on their combined army and police pensions and Dartford became an early posting station where rapid experience could be gained before the men moved on to other areas with, perhaps, slightly less concentrated policework. Greater responsibilities became common, as did Acting Sergeant duties when no other sergeant was available. To take on an Acting task usually required that constable to have passed the sergeant's examination but, in the absence of any such high-flying candidate, my minor seniority took precedence. Taking overall control of a major traffic accident or other incident at aged 22 years with a trio of totally inexperienced trainees wondering what to do with a traffic cone, was not uncommon and experience of many varied emergencies and unlikely situations were quickly attained.

An area of experience which remains memorable for me is my attendance at incidents caused by violence even though when the first information was available, violence was probably not initially suspected.

This is the unknown factor which makes police work a real adrenaline-rush for so many policemen.

One minute an officer can be day-dreaming about his next cup of tea, or Arsenal's chances next Saturday, the next minute a call is received to go to a location and deal with something.

It may be a serious assault, a suicide, a road traffic accident, or any one of countless reasons for requiring a policeman. It makes police work out of the ordinary.

With only a few months service, I turned up for night duty at 9.45pm and found a strange atmosphere in the station. I asked, jokingly, if there had been a murder, to which the reply was, "Yes. Guess who is doing first relief at the scene?"

So, yours truly, accompanied by a pack of cheese sandwiches, was conveyed in the CID car to Stone, where I was led into a terraced house and told by a detective sergeant that I was to guard the scene of the crime until relieved at 7am the next morning.

The story was that a lady in her forties had been stabbed to death earlier that day and found, lying on the kitchen floor, by a family friend when she called on the address some few hours later.

The chief suspect was the victim's nephew and he might return, so I was not to turn the light on. If he did return, I was to call for assistance.

I was then left at the house on my own, with only my sandwiches and torch for comfort.

Time passed whilst I listened to the radio in the darkness, although I was dreading midnight when the BBC ceased its transmission for the night. Would I be able to receive Radio Luxembourg on this tiny radio? I hated the thought that the remainder of the shift could be endured in this house of death without some form of entertainment.

By 11pm I had eaten my sandwiches. Dare I go into the kitchen? I hadn't been told, but I was assuming that the body had been removed to the mortuary. Fortunately, it had.

After some consideration, I decided that, as the Scenes of Crimes officer had completed his task, I could go in and see if I could make a cup of tea.

I went into the kitchen and immediately saw the amount of blood that had drained out of the poor lady before she had died.

A dark pool of vermilion fluid had spread across the floor tiles and disappeared beneath some cupboards. Drag marks had increased the spread and there were sprays of blood up the wall and over the working surface by the sink.

In due respect to the poor lady, I simply felt that it would not be right to carry out even such a simple domestic task as making a cup of tea where such an evil deed had been perpetrated only a few hours earlier. I went back into the front room and there I sat in silence until 7 am when the early turn relief arrived.

They wondered why no-one had been to see me throughout the night shift and "Why was I so pale. Was I feeling unwell?" It was only later that I considered as to how it would have been possible to summon assistance if the nephew had turned up.

There had been no telephone at the house. Should I have blown my whistle and hoped . . .

One fine afternoon I was driving a policewoman round Dartford whilst she made her calls which pertained to the particular additional duties of lady officers of those days. Jane did not hold a driver's licence and relied on colleagues to convey her to her tasks.

We were on our way back to the police station when we received a call over the radio that she was required to attend, straight away, at an address at Swanley. Her specific services were needed.

There was no indication what the problem was but that we should make all haste there.

About fifteen minutes later we arrived at the address which was in a rural area.

The Swanley 999 response car was parked outside and a sergeant was leaning against it smoking a cigarette. He came over to us as we got out and I looked over the low hedge into the front garden of the house. A young female was lying by the front door and there was blood everywhere.

Without any obvious tension in his voice, the sergeant said to Jane, "We have had a murder here. Pop into the house and make the mother a cup of tea, will you. Be careful where you walk."

The professional attitude of the Swanley sergeant was still the coolest I had ever encountered at that time.

A short while later the CID murder team from headquarters arrived to take over, and I spent the rest of the afternoon being an obedient runner for any senior officer who cared to shout at me.

The attacker of the poor girl who had met her demise had been an ex-boyfriend who had taken offence at the girl's choice of new boyfriend and stabbed her through the neck as she arrived home.

It seems that the knife severed the carotid artery in her neck. The spurting fountain of blood created by the arterial pressure within her body would have diminished to a trickle within ten seconds, at which time she would already have been dead.

Her mother heard the commotion but was unable to help her daughter. She was able to dial 999 after which she passed out with shock.

The Swanley sergeant initially believed that he had two bodies when he arrived but was relieved to find the mother uninjured and able to explain what she knew.

The assailant had left the scene after the attack and it transpired that he had then gone back to his home near Sidcup, where he was later found by the Metropolitan Police behind the locked toilet door having committed suicide with the same knife that he had used for the original horrendous attack.

Following a successful investigation into something as serious as murder, it is usual for the investigating officers to have a "de-briefing" so that factors within the case can be reviewed and, if necessary, recorded for future benefit. In this case, the de-briefing was held at Dartford police station bar to which all officers involved were invited.

This was to be my first experience of triumphalism whereby the investigators were all extremely happy about the conclusion but I was subdued. A beautiful young lady had her life taken away by a despicable act of vengeance that had been totally out of proportion to reason and we were celebrating the timely suicide of her attacker and the simplicity of the future inquests.

It was not my idea of a cause for celebration.

CHAPTER 12

Time for a Move

IN 1966 I had considered that my previous specialist experience in photography, both as a professionally taught studio, medical and general photographer, and as an experienced darkroom technician, would stand me in good stead for a position in the specialist areas of Scenes of Crime work and I sought the necessary course of action to get a transfer request underway.

Following discussions with my family regarding my planned future in the Kent Police Force, and with supervisory officers to establish official procedure, I managed to get a couple of hours in the muster room where officers were allowed time to complete official reports. I requested some plain report paper and carbon paper from the clerk and carefully worded my application in triplicate to Headquarters on the ancient Imperial typewriter, and had it checked by Sergeant Wills. I then re-typed it with his suggested comments and re-submitted it.

The duty inspector had a look, corrected it to what he thought it should be and it came back to me for retyping.

That done, it went to the chief inspector, who demanded that it be retyped with his suggested wording, leading to further delay before, finally, the report left Dartford for Headquarters where I hoped that all my work, both in photography and in marathon typing, would receive a positive response and that my future as a beat bobby would end with a position in the scientific branch.

A month later, the report came winging back to my tray. Disappointingly, my request had been dismissed, citing the excuse that my experience counted for nothing as they "prefer to train their own experts in that area".

An analogy would be a chef who had joined the army would be sent to the motor pool, whilst the lorry driver recruit would be given a recipe book and tall white hat.

On that same theme, my subsequent application to be a specialist traffic officer—with only 18 months experience of a full car licence—was approved immediately, pending a driving assessment.

A week later I was called to the Kent Police Driving School, which was located alongside the main Headquarters complex at Maidstone.

I travelled there on the remaining police Velocette 150cc motorcycle, dressed in my full wet-weather gear because of the torrential rain, arriving at Maidstone soaked through, with water pouring out of my boots, thoroughly miserable and cold—hardly in the best mood to undergo a severe test of my driving skills.

I got myself a cup of tea at the canteen and was trying to dry myself out when a sergeant-instructor came into the dining room and called for me.

I answered my name and when he saw me, he said, "You're all wet. That doesn't bode well for a traffic man!" He laughed at his own humour, threw me a set of keys and said, "We'll take the Wolseley 6/110. Ever driven one before?" I told him that I hadn't but didn't let on that I had never even seen a 6/110 before.

The sun was at last coming out as we entered the yard and I saw the gleaming, black, brand new Wolesley car waiting for me. The thought of being able to get in and drive such a quality car gave me a huge thrill.

"It's a 2912cc, S6 overhead valve engine with an 83mm bore and 89mm stroke, 120 horses, SU twin carbs and a top of just over 100, nought to sixty in a shade under 13, Borg Warner overdrive—but you won't be needing that today. We're not gonna be cruisin'!"

I just thought to myself, "Oooh! Black car—expensive!"

I got behind the very upright steering wheel and, as I had been warned to do, performed a basic cockpit drill. This entailed identifying all the controls and checking the levels on the dashboard.

"Let's do it then," said the instructor and I obediently started the engine, selected first gear, released the clutch pedal—and stalled.

Fortunately, that was the only part of the drive that did not go to plan and I was able to drive around the roads and lanes of mid-Kent for the next 45 minutes without mishap or scares.

It was as if the general public was keeping completely out of my way, but that could have been because the car was so obviously a Wolesley police traffic patrol car!

Having received a positive response to the drive, the instructor, having cleverly noticed that I had arrived at police headquarters in motorcycle gear, asked me if I also wanted to have a suitability test for motorcycles.

I didn't want to miss out on the opportunity and, twenty minutes later, I was screaming along behind a waterproof-clad senior motorcyclist of the driving school, he on a Triumph 750cc machine and myself on a BSA 650cc machine. I was given to understand that if I was to be able to keep up with Crazy Colin, as he was known, that would also be regarded as a pass, and qualify me for suitable further training.

Despite my BSA motorcycle having a very loose central stand that scraped along the ground, he failed to shake me off and I passed this test as well.

I later found out that the student's bike was never quite to the high standard of the instructor's bike on these suitability tests. All part of the enjoyment, I suppose.

I returned to Dartford in a rainstorm, soaking every part of me that had remained dry earlier in the day but feeling elated that I would soon be a member of Kent Traffic Division.

Two days later I was tucked up in bed with the worst cold that I had experienced in years.

During the 1960s, Kent Police had five traffic areas covering the county's roads. Number 1 Area Traffic Office (ATO) was based at Maidstone Headquarters and was the biggest by manpower and numbers of vehicles.

Number 3 ATO covered north-east Kent, and was located at Nackington, south of the City of Canterbury. Number 4 ATO was based at Seabrook, near Folkestone, and covered the south east part of Kent including Romney Marsh, Ashford and the east Kentish Weald. 5 ATO was the smallest area and was based at Tonbridge, covering the county from Tunbridge Wells to the Metropolitan Police border.

Number 2 Traffic Area was based in the Medway Towns at Rochester and was the area to which I was detailed to serve in 1966.

It covered the parts of north Kent between Dartford and Sittingbourne including the Medway Towns of Chatham, Rochester and Gillingham.

The police garage, more accurately known as the Area Traffic Office HQ, was based underneath the old railway arches in Corporation Street, at Rochester, near Rochester Bridge. It was similar to other archway premises, many of which are still to be seen in south-east London, where the railway lines are elevated some ten metres above ground level. The archways beneath the tracks are walled-in to form separate units.

At Rochester several arches had been linked together to form a series of treble car-width garages for cars, vans, motorcycles and the area workshops.

The continual rumble of the trains as they passed over the top of the arches meant that conversation stopped in mid-sentence—and then re-started again after the train had passed.

At the rear of this series of arches was a long corridor linking the various offices for muster, senior officers' hideaway, administration duties and kitchen facilities (where the teapot and frying pan were kept!).

Behind the kitchen there was derelict ground covered with buddleia and the largest pile of disposed-of tea leaves that anyone has ever encountered. I was sure that if there was an award in the Guinness Book of Records for piles of tea leaves, this pile would have won with honours. Some 40 years of teapot contents, disposed of through the kitchen window twenty times a day, had created a pile almost as high as the windowsill. Policemen do drink an awful lot of tea . . .

The camaraderie of traffic officers in those days I found to be extremely close and friendly.

On a number of occasions, the members of the late turn, whose duty roster concluded at 10pm, would still be at the muster area at 11pm, perhaps playing darts or cribbage, when a call would be heard from a night-duty officer requesting urgent assistance on the main A2 or other major road.

Immediately, someone would answer the radio in the communications office and proffer help from the lads still present at the Area office.

Due attendance would be made if required and no thought would be made to claiming overtime for these emergency calls.

One such call that came in late one night was a report of an overturned goods vehicle on the A2 at Cobham where the crew of the patrol car attending had realised that considerable assistance would be required. One of the sergeants agreed that six of us would attend in three patrol cars to divert traffic and assist in sorting out the resulting chaos which was extensive.

A 32 ton heavy goods vehicle being operated on behalf of Marks & Spencer was on its side across the A2, completely blocking the road. Two other private cars had also been involved but were not creating too much additional problem.

An extra consideration was that the load had broken out of the lorry and it was everywhere! It was fresh fruit, of all types, that had been on its way for delivery to stores country-wide. The driver had contacted his depot from a nearby telephone box and was told that a senior manager would be coming out.

An hour later, the said manager deemed that the entire load was a total write-off and instructed us to take whatever action we could to dispose of the pallets of boxes.

Kent police officers readily applied their minds to this urgent matter and as many vehicles as could be spared were called to assist. The lorry could not be raised before the contents of the trailer were removed and I have to say that a considerable quantity of fresh fruit was, the following morning, neatly stacked in the archway garages at Corporation Street. Indeed, there were so many broken/damaged boxes that some patrol cars had to be parked outside.

Much of the fruit was delivered the next day to various old people's homes and similar establishments and there were a large number of police wives making jam for the next few days.

This camaraderie between Number 2 Area officers changed for the worse a couple of years later when the garage was incorporated with the new Rochester police station, with much stricter discipline imposed upon us all. Making things bigger does not always make them better.

The stationing of traffic personnel in the same building as sub-divisional personnel was always going to cause friction and this proved to be the case.

Traffic police had an advantage over their sub-divisional counterparts in the area of radio communications.

The traffic patrol cars were fitted with radios which actually worked. Communication systems had been, and continued to be problematical in the county due to the distances between the mobiles and the transmitters. For some reason the larger cars and batteries of traffic patrol cars resulted in substantially better reception with fewer black-spots.

Kent is a fairly hilly county, with the North Downs crossing it like a spine from west to east. Transmission masts were located on the highest points but other topographical features and tall buildings meant that the reception received by the sub-divisional cars was not as reliable as the better-quality reception of the traffic car radios.

Kent police radio was divided into two separate VHF radio channels controlled from the operations room at Force HQ, Maidstone. The civilian operators sat alongside each other on a raised dais at their separate control panels with one directing east Kent and the other, west Kent.

In this way all mobiles could be directed to incidents and could communicate with each other.

From 1967, UHF personal radios started appearing in a rather lamentable way, because they were an untried facility but technical advances over the coming years did much to improve the system. Being of differing bandwidths, there was no common interchange between the UHF and VHF which created operational difficulties.

The countywide VHF communications became busier with more and more police vehicles being fitted with them and using them regularly. So much so that the rules emanating from FHQ led to a strange thing called Radio Procedure and an American import–the Ten Code.

In those days of black & white television, there was an American cop programme called *Highway Patrol* starring Broderick Crawford as an overweight sheriff. His response to messages was always "10-4", meaning in the American jargon that the message had been received and would be acted upon.

It seems that senior officers considered that the adoption of the 10-Code by Kent Police would enhance good procedure and stop a lot of unofficial chat which tended to go on, especially at night.

Before this new code system was introduced the patrols used to pass their messages in normal speech that everyone could understand. Now, with the 10-Code, we would all be able to converse in a rapid, secret language that the public would have no idea about . . .

The 10-Code was also used with the full NATO phonetic alphabet—even though the number of syllables exceeded those of the original letter (e.g. A=Alpha, I=India, U=Uniform, etc.).

The basic codes were as follows:

10-1—On watch

10-2—Contact station by landline

10-3—Return to station

10-4—At refreshments, etc, etc.

All patrol cars were given call signs that identified, a) the home station, and b) the type of police vehicle.

The home station also had a static radio set in the sergeant's office whose call sign identified the division and station.

On traffic division the home station, or base, was in our case T2 or, phonetically "Tango 2". The cars were identified as "Tango Bravo 1" (Bravo being the letter of the division where No.2 Area Traffic Office (ATO) was located).

All this strict radio procedure became very tedious and was subject to a degree of humour at times.

A further facet of police radios was that we could only hear what was said by the operator because replies were covered by pips.

There is a technical word for this state, known as half-duplex, but it could be over-ridden by the operator who pressed a talk-through switch to enable cars to talk to each other directly. Of course, any member of the public who illegally tuned-in to police wavelengths when talk-through was enabled could hear all our conversations.

One day the sergeant at 2ATO wanted one of his men, who was in patrol car call-sign TB2, to contact him. He first had to get the Maidstone operator to put the radio into talk-through mode. The ensuing transmissions were then made which went down in traffic police folklore.

2 Area: "Tango 2, Tango 2, over . . ."

HQ: "Go ahead Tango 2"

2 Area: "Tango 2, Tango 2. Can I have talk-through with Tango Bravo 2."

HQ: "Tango Bravo 2, Tango Bravo 2, over . . ."

TB2: "Tango Bravo 2".

HQ: "Tango Bravo 2, Tango Bravo 2. Talk through with Tango 2 . . . Tango 2, Tango 2. Tango Bravo 2 will talk through with Tango 2. Go ahead Tango 2 . . ."

2Area: "Tango Bravo 2, Tango Bravo 2. This is Tango 2 over . . ."

TB2: "Tango 2, Tango 2. This is Tango Bravo 2 receiving you."

2Area: "Tango Bravo 2, Tango Bravo 2. Will you 10-2, T2?"

TB2: "Tango 2, Tango 2, I will 10-2 Tango 2 in 02"

2Area: "Oh dear. So much for brevity with strict radio procedure."

The other advantage of having a call-sign commencing with Tango Bravo was that they shared a common call-sign with the space vehicles on the *Thunderbirds* animation series that was so popular on television around the 1960s. This coincidence led to the 2 Area traffic cars being nicknamed Thunderbird 1, etc, etc.

My own allocated patrol car was usually TB4 and we frequently signed on with the control room with the exclamation, "Thunderbird 4 is GO".

A childish aberration but bits of harmless humour always made the day pass more easily.

After the pubs and clubs had closed and all good people were tucked up in their beds, police radio traffic was usually at a very low level.

By 4 o'clock in the morning several minutes could go by without a murmur and some of the operators were kind enough to place a radio tuned into the Light Programme (now Radio2) against the microphone to provide the sleepy night duty officers with soothing music. This did not, of course, preclude any urgent calls from being made in either direction.

On many such quiet occasions the operator would cancel the half-duplex mode and leave the radio on talk-through mode so that minor messages could be passed between mobiles and/or their home station.

My first Saturday afternoon as a traffic patrol officer was in company with Peter, who was also my nextdoor neighbour.

Peter was an experienced patrol officer who held a Class I Advanced Driver's Certificate and had many other traffic-related qualifications.

He was a large man who rolled his own cigarettes whilst steering with his stomach—a well-practiced skill which is not recommended to the general public.

We had left the traffic garage just after 1400hrs and I had the honour of driving a white Austin Westminster three litre patrol car, call sign Thunderbird 3 (sorry, Tango Bravo 3), into the town centre of Rochester and on towards Chatham.

It was just then that a call came over the police radio asking for units to respond to a serious injury accident that had just occurred in a distant community some ten miles to the north of Rochester. Peter acknowledged the call and, as I was the junior driver, I pulled over to the kerb and stopped, where we changed seats.

I was then to experience my first advanced drive in operational mode from one of the best drivers on our area. With his driving seat pulled up so close to the steering wheel that his stomach was in continuous contact with it, Peter drove through Rochester High Street at a steady, but progressive speed, across Rochester Bridge and into Strood.

Our patrol car was fitted with an electronically controlled, chromium-plated bell mounted ahead of the front grill of the car, which I sounded continuously and traffic seemed to melt away from our path. We left Strood along the main road to the Isle of Grain, and our speed increased to nearly 100 miles-per-hour.

We simply flew past the ambulance which was also in attendance, and which itself was travelling at emergency speed.

There was a point along the route to the scene where the main road crossed a railway line by means of a large road-bridge. Not exactly a hump-back but one which makes a car go light at speed. Peter warned me to hold on tight, and we did actually take off on the far side of the bridge.

Our arrival at the scene, which was a serious injury accident between an elderly pedestrian and a motorcycle rider, was timed by our control room at twelve minutes. To travel twelve miles, including the journey through the centre of Rochester and Strood, in such a short time on a Saturday afternoon, was quite a feat.

At no time during this call did I feel the slightest concern for our safety. The car was at all times perfectly balanced and being driven in total accord with the manual.

I hoped that, one day, my expertise in car control would be up to that high standard.

Driver training was an area of police work which was given a high priority in Kent.

On joining Traffic Division, officers were given driving suitability tests by expert examiners, following which they would be designated as Class 5 or 6.

My initial test on that earlier wet day had classified me as a Class 5 driver and motorcyclist. That classification entitled the holder to be behind the wheel of a traffic division patrol car whilst in the company of a trained driver. Any emergency work was then taken over by the trained driver.

Once accepted for traffic division, the earliest priority was to get onto a full five-week residential driving course at the Kent Police Driver Training School, one of the highest-standard police driving schools in the United Kingdom.

We in Kent were lucky to have such a driving school based at our force headquarters at Maidstone.

It was a residential establishment and regarded as a very close second to the Metropolitan Police Driving School at Hendon, which was world-renowned for its reputation in turning out skilled and confident drivers.

Whilst Hendon concentrated on training pupils on town and city roads, Kent's reputation was for open road and faster speed training.

Maidstone took pupils from all over southeast England on various courses ranging from the standard car and motorcycle driving courses, where pupils attained Class 3 or Class 4 qualifications up to the advanced courses, where Classes 1 and 2 could be obtained.

The driving school was under the control of a chief inspector, assisted by an inspector. The instructors were either of sergeant rank or were civilian instructors with traffic police experience, they having retired from traffic division and gone straight into driver training.

All the driving school instructors were, therefore, skilled and experienced advanced traffic-division drivers who exhibited their abilities by giving Class 1 demonstration drives before allowing their charges to sit behind the wheel.

Additionally, the driving school provided traffic-related courses in road traffic law and in specialist subjects such as vehicle technology and tachograph calibration courses.

Later, the school was to become known for its accident investigation courses where scientific theory in vehicle technology and braking science were accepted by the courts.

The general public were also able to avail themselves of the skills and experience of these instructors through the force's "Better Driving" courses.

These were in the form of an evening school. Members of the general public signed up for these courses for a reasonable fee. They were then invited to join a series of evening lectures in the classroom where police driving theory was taught. Emphasis was always on safety and planning ahead for hazards and other dangers.

The course ended on a designated weekend when one of the instructors took three students in a high-powered police driving-school car and demonstrated his advanced driving skills to them.

It was quite a scary and very sobering experience for many drivers who had never been driven so fast and yet so safely over public roads. The courses were always well over-subscribed and it was hoped that driving skills could be built on those experiences.

Sadly, even though public support and the general popularity for experiencing police driver training remained high, this course no longer exists because of the demise of the dedicated driving school and, of course, costs. The only way to get a somewhat similar experience today is to exceed the speed limit by 7 miles-per-hour, and then pay £125 for the privilege. You do not get the weekend drive, unfortunately.

I underwent my standard course of driving instruction in late 1967 and managed to attain a Class 3 qualification.

The first two weeks of the course had rammed home every page of the police driver's bible—*The Police Manual of Car Control*, as well as every word of the *Highway Code*.

Examinations were not made easy and it was possible to fail after two weeks and be returned to one's police station without appeal. The last three weeks were devoted to practical driving skills with three pupils, in a high powered car, to each instructor. Routes took us over all types of road—urban, country, open and dualled.

With the driving-school cars there was a strict discipline in force.

At the start of every day the nominated pupil driver first walked round the car to examine for external damage of any kind.

Tyre pressures were always checked with a manual gauge and the treads were examined for stones or damage.

The bonnet was lifted and visual checks were made of the oil level, radiator water level, brake fluid level, windscreen washer level and any other points regarding pipes, tubes, battery and associated working parts.

He then took his seat behind the wheel and, with the assistance of another pupil, checked all lights, indicators, and screen wash/wipe operations.

A full cockpit drill was then carried out verbally, when each control and instrument was identified and checked so as to prove to the instructor that the pupil was now familiar with that particular model of car. After all, there is nothing worse than giving another motorist a loud windscreen washer warning instead of a horn sound!

Thus familiar with that model of car, the engine would be started and checks made on dash board warning lights and fuel level. Then, and only then, was first gear engaged and the actual art of driving commenced.

The two non-participant pupils were expected to remain calmly on the back seat and stay totally silent throughout the drive—even though the desire to scream out loud at some foolish overtaking manoeuvre might be very tempting.

All school cars were equipped with full lap and diagonal seatbelts, even though the law in those days did not demand it. Occupants were obliged to wear them correctly at all times when on the public roads.

Each stint behind the wheel was of around 20 to 30 minutes and took the car around the roads of mid-Kent where the pupil received instruction on observation, safety zones, correct choice of speed and positioning for passing manoeuvres.

At a convenient point there would be a break of some minutes during which an inquisition would be held. This inquisition, led by the instructor, would cover virtually every inch of the route taken, with amazing recollection. Criticism was usually very high at the start of the course, with the other pupils allowed to add their points of view.

These latter comments lessened over the days because it tended to destroy friendships!

The intensity of the training was very high and a session of driving always contained at least one incident worth arguing about.

Pupils would then change over and the next driver would go through the standard checks until the instructor was satisfied.

In weeks 4 and 5, checks were only carried out at the start of the day's tuition. Each pupil had their allocated driving periods and at the end of the day, the car's recorded mileage was usually around 200 miles. That was 60-70 miles per pupil, carried out under extreme pressure whilst assimilating the driver skills required for the final drive.

If the back of your shirt was not soaking wet with perspiration at the completion of the stint, there was insufficient effort being put into the drive.

The instructors continually assessed each pupil's drive and those perspiration levels were kept very high. With the training came confidence and an appreciation of car control that equipped the pupil with skills which he would, hopefully, retain and take advantage of in the future.

The final drive took place on the Thursday of the last week.

The examination car was prepared early and stood, gleaming, on the garage forecourt. Pupils in turn were called forward to the driver's seat and were joined by the chief inspector of the driving school who would be conducting the test.

The sergeant instructor would sit quietly in the back seat, directly behind the pupil, so as to be another set of testing eyes.

A simple cockpit drill would be performed, as much for the pupil as for the examiner, because it was possible that the pupil had not actually driven the final test car before that moment. The route would be outlined by the chief inspector and would usually cover some 40 miles of road, to include town, country lane, and the faster open roads. All 30 and 40 limit speed-restricted areas were to be correctly adhered to, but the white sign with a diagonal black bar across it—the National Speed Limit Applies sign—was known to police driving-school pupils as the "Go! Board".

The Home Office gave special dispensation to police training vehicles to exceed those limits whilst the pupil was under instruction or being tested.

The pupil was required to obey all other traffic regulations and to make progress with all dispatch, subject to due consideration for those public drivers who were not watching their mirrors and might have a seizure at being passed so quickly. In other words, to drive at emergency-call speed but without using the blue lights, bells and bright headlights.

A further requirement of the test was for the pupil, when invited by the examiner, to commence a running commentary whilst driving. This is an art which had been practiced over the period of instruction but is a difficult skill, requiring the tongue and brain to keep up with the road speed.

One frequently described "approaching a left-hand bend" when the car had already passed around the bend at fairly high speed and was now heading for the next right-hand bend.

I recall that, when I was under test, we entered Tenterden High Street and came to a stop in a traffic jam and the chief inspector said "Right-oh, start your commentary." What a dirty trick. All I could do was outline that the controls were operating correctly and that warning lights were off, the handbrake was engaged and the car ahead of me was stationary. Still, it did show a sense of humour and he later give me another chance on the open road.

Besides a high level of observation and speed awareness, one of the major aspects of driving is safe overtaking.

There was a saying that "the second car in the line of moving traffic causes the queue". When driving along an open road and you, the driver, catch up with a slower-moving vehicle, it is an indication that your average speed has been greater than that of the vehicle ahead, be it a car, lorry, tractor or bicycle. This situation suggests that your next action should be to plan to pass that vehicle at the earliest opportunity. After all, you are now the second vehicle in the queue.

Great importance was placed by the instructors on the skill of overtaking. It is probably the most dangerous aspect of progressive driving and requires observation, positioning and an awareness of the situation that the average motorist will never have been taught.

Observation will tell the driver whether the road ahead (traffic flows, bends, parked cars, etc) might allow for the act of overtaking to be carried out. If, and only if, that observation indicates that there will be an opportunity, the driver will take up a position that will give him a maximum view of all likely hazards, including his rear view situation.

Maximum advantage is taken of the view to the offside of the target vehicle, including vehicles in view and of those vehicles that can be expected to come into view from a blind area ahead. The correct gear for the speed is selected and, when totally satisfied as to the safety of the manoeuvre, a final mirror check is performed and the action will take place with necessary dispatch.

To this action must be added any signal that would benefit any other road user, then to pass the target vehicle giving as much room for safety as appropriate, and to return to the correct side of the road in a normal manner.

This is all very well when written down but the actual practice can only be perfected by practice and skilled criticism from experienced instructors or highly qualified drivers.

The above clearly illustrates the reason for attending a school of this standard. Overtaking usually requires the driver to use the "wrong" side of the road. It is dangerous over there!

Further skills that were taught by the school were in low speed manoeuvring, parking, and the art of control of skidding on the large skidpan adjacent to the garages.

It wasn't until attending the advanced course that there was an examination on skid control.

In that, the pupil had to choreograph a two minute programme of controlled skidding around the tyre barriers located on the skidpan. On the standard course, we were only allowed to play.

It is sad to relate that the Kent driving school no longer operates residential courses. Indeed, the location of the skidpan is now located beneath the frozen-food department of a supermarket.

The final skill was in car cleaning, which was done in the last hour of the day, repeated daily, and always performed with our best efforts—or else we had to do it again. There were no automatic car washes available for police use in the 1960s.

Vehicles allocated to traffic division usually had a police-life of three to four years and were disposed of through trade car auctions with frequently in excess of 150,000 miles indicated on the odometer.

Many cars were in use 24 hours a day, 7 days a week at some traffic areas. One hundred miles per 8 hour shift was normal, meaning that 1500-2000 miles a week was possible.

Anyone buying such an ex police-owned vehicle might expect the high mileage to be detrimental but the servicing intervals had been strictly adhered to with any defects being dealt with quickly and professionally by dedicated police fitters in the area garages.

The high-speed use of these cars ensured that the engines were always clean inside because of the high temperatures burning off excess carbon. These conditions, together with generally sympathetic driving methods, meant that they were often seen as bargains within the trade.

The public may think that fast driving is unsympathetic to the vehicle being driven but the police teaching was to be at one with the car, always anticipating the next gear change or braking action.

A further example is the rule to dip the clutch when passing over uneven surfaces, such as the railway level crossing (which is generally anything but level) so as to disengage the driven wheels from the transmission, thus preventing strain on the clutch and associated engine components. It all helps to save undue wear and tear on the hard-driven cars.

The police driving-school cars tended to be rather older than the area traffic cars because their usage was mainly during the daytime hours, five days a week. In addition, the external care matched the mechanical care and, on being sold, offered the very best in value to anyone prepared to use an ex-cop car.

Mind you, the blue lights and bell were removed before sale of the traffic patrol vehicles!

The results of the final Thursday driving tests were announced on the morning of the last day of the course when certificates were issued.

These certificates, on A4 card, signed by the Chief Constable and Chief Instructor were something tangible to take away from the driving school and I still have all of those documents that I received over the years.

The marques of traffic cars in those days were mainly Austin Westminster, Wolesley 110, Ford Zephyr, Humber Super Snipe Estates and, later, Jaguar 340s. They were initially black and the warning system was a large chromed bell mounted on the front bumper.

During the late 1960s, replacement cars were changed to white and the twin-note air horn mounted on the roof became the favourite toy.

I recall with much pleasure the first time I drove through the length of Dartford High Street on a crowded Saturday afternoon on my way to a serious accident to the west of the town.

No-one had experienced air horn warnings before, always having had to respond (or not) to the clanging bell.

My arrival in Dartford High Street with the loud resonant tones of the brand new Italian-made Fiamm air horns echoing against the tall buildings on either side of the High Street was akin to the story of Moses and the Red Sea parting. I have never seen people move so fast.

The air horns did have one amusing downside. In winter, on patrol during snow, the fronts of the air horns, being cornet-shaped, collected snow inside them. On throwing the switch to sound the horns, there would be a wheezing sound and then, if you were lucky, two ice-cream shaped snowballs would shoot out of the front of the horns and slide down the windscreen, followed by the resonant dooo-daaa, as if in relief.

It was 1968 that, for some reason initially unbeknown to anyone of lower rank, traffic division took delivery of some Jaguar 340 saloons.

Then we found out that our chief constable had just taken delivery of a new official car—a Jaguar Mk10, now more correctly known as the 420G.

So that's why we now had Jaguars! Traffic men were particularly cynical about such events.

These patrol Jaguars were painted white, which was a shame because the black Jaguar was always a thing of great beauty, but they were something else when it came to travelling at speed.

We had two of these vehicles at the Rochester garage and only first class drivers were allowed to drive in excess of 80 miles-per-hour. This meant that we lowly Class 3 drivers had to relinquish the wheel if a call was received as there was always a Class 1 driver with the car.

In the early hours of a beautiful summer night, I had been cruising around the Medway towns at the wheel of the Jaguar and was about to drive onto the industrial estate at Gillingham, when we received a call to intercept a vehicle involved in the kidnapping of a young child, where the welfare of the child was feared for.

My partner, sad to say, had been dozing in the passenger seat and therefore not in any position to concentrate on driving at speed straightaway. He took the decision to allow me to drive to Northfleet, a route that would take us along the newly completed M2 motorway and fast dual carriageway roads.

With his instruction, I built up my speed and I was amazed to see the speedometer of the car register almost 140 miles-per-hour at one point.

From that time on, I have enjoyed the thrill of driving at speed, whilst having great respect for the obvious dangers inherent in so doing.

Oh, yes. We were able to intercept the kidnapper and, with the assistance of one of the town cars, return the child to its mother.

Whatever the reason for it, the chief constable was soon to re-allocate his big Jaguar 420G to traffic division. It was painted in the white livery, fitted out with blue lights and emergency equipment, and went to the No. 3 (Canterbury) area garage where it was used for mainly motorway patrol on the newly-opened M2 motorway.

It didn't last very long because the ride was so somnambulistic that at 4am one morning the two patrolmen in it dozed off—still travelling at some considerable speed—and wrote it off by testing the rolling resistance of the roof whilst driving upside down along the carriageway.

On the subject of dozing off whilst driving at night, there is the well known case of the two officers driving down the M2 from Chatham towards the Medway Bridge. The passenger was dozing in his seat when he was awoken by the sound of gravel being thrown up against the underside of the patrol car. He opened his eyes and saw that the patrol car was driving down the hard shoulder at 70 miles-per-hour, very, very, close to the metal barrier on the left hand side. He looked at the driver who appeared to have closed his eyes.

"What ARE you doing?" shouted the passenger.

The driver opened his eyes and just said, "Oh, I thought you were driving."

He regained the carriageway and continued on as if nothing had happened. They never patrolled together again after that episode.

Being a member of traffic division in those days was regarded, not entirely correctly, as a step up from the routine of sub-divisional policing.

Traffic officers tended to take a pride in their vehicles, being allocated a specific car in which to carry out their patrols.

The usual ratio at our traffic garage was four officers to one patrol car with one officer, usually of senior service, having the prime responsibility for the upkeep and cleanliness of the vehicle. In that way, the officers retained a modicum of pride and generally kept the insides clear of cigarette ash and sweet papers.

If the exterior of the car was soiled after the shift, it was washed down and leathered off. Regardless of the cleanliness, or otherwise, of the bodywork, the windows were always cleaned AFTER the duty period finished, and the fuel and oil levels were always topped up so that everything was ready for the next person to drive.

There was a certain cachet in being able to wear the single silver button stitched onto the right arm of the uniform jacket. This was used to attach the starched white sleevelet that was donned by the traffic division driver to make clearer the arm signals that were given out of the window for the benefit of other motorists.

The only hand signals given by motorists in the 21st Century seem to be of the coarse variety from inside the windscreen and tend to aggravate, not help, other drivers.

Above all, the traffic cop had to be good at talking to people and have the right manner to engage with drivers who had broken the driving laws, either through carelessness or deliberately.

The more satisfying cases were when someone had committed a clear offence in front of the patrol car and, after being dealt with, had accepted the consequences in full realisation that there was a reason for the police action.

I understand that things have changed since those heady days.

On patrol one morning, I was watching eastbound traffic about to enter extended roadworks on the A2 at Northfleet where there was a 40 mph speed limit in force for the next 8 miles.

It was a misty, damp, day and the road was wet. An American-made Ford Mustang came into my view from London, travelling at high speed.

The driver obviously failed to see my large white patrol car at the side of the road and roared past me towards Canterbury. I immediately joined the traffic, chased after this car and found that I was unable to close the distance between us, even though my speed frequently exceeded 80 mph.

The Mustang driver was seemingly oblivious to the speed limit, and traffic around him, and I was unable to pull him over until reaching the M2 motorway near Rochester, some nine miles after the chase began.

I asked him for an explanation as to why he had been driving so fast; to which he replied that he was late for an appointment.

When pressed further, he admitted that his appointment was at the Quarter Sessions Court at Canterbury where he was to answer a charge of dangerous driving by way of excess speed. He even saw the irony of the matter before continuing his journey to court in possession of an additional "Notice of Intended Prosecution" safely tucked away in his wallet.

During the mid 1960s, the first Race Relations Act came into force. I regret that there was an occasion when I was advised by a senior officer that I had transgressed this law, even though I disagreed vehemently that I had been acting in a racist manner.

I had been watching traffic approaching a particularly dangerous area of the A2 near Northfleet where double white lines controlled the moving traffic and warned east-bound traffic not to overtake on the approach to a blind brow.

A Vauxhall saloon car was then seen to come past the continuous line of slower-moving traffic, completely on the wrong side of the system and causing opposing west-bound traffic to take avoiding action.

It was one of the most blatant offences against the double white line law that I have come across, either before or since. I went after the offending car and, after a short chase, stopped the driver. I walked to the car with my clipboard in hand, ready to report the driver straight away.

It was always regarded as good practice to make up your mind what action you were going to take before speaking to the offender. In that way, you cannot be swayed by one of many reasons which might occur to alter that early decision. Examples of the type of thing that I have experienced are the £5 note in the Driver's Licence, the beautiful blonde driver with a short skirt and fluttering eye lids, various sob stories about how late they are, etc.

On reaching the driver's window, I saw that the driver was a West Indian male with another West Indian male in the passenger seat. There was still no immediate problem as far as I was concerned. The driver would be reported for the driving offence and I would ask to see his driving documents and issue a form for their production if they were not to hand.

From that moment on matters took a turn for the worse. The driver refused to listen to my description of what I had seen, with both men raising their voices in an aggressive manner.

The driver also said that I had only stopped him because he was black. No matter how I approached them, they failed to see reason.

I then got fed up with the prevarication and changed my tack.

I told the driver that I now required to examine his vehicle in respect of lights, brakes and so forth. This is a power that any police officer in uniform has if he is satisfied that the car is being used on the public highway and the driver is present.

At that moment, another police colleague pulled up and the two males eventually calmed down.

Additional offences concerning the vehicle's lighting and braking system were discovered and, instead of merely receiving a summons for the white-line offence, the driver was warned he would be prosecuted for additional offences in relation to the mechanical condition of his car. These additional summonses would reflect his poor attitude as well as his vehicular defects and were issued with no regard whatsoever to his colour. I would have dealt with any driver the same way.

I gave him a form to produce his driving documents and, satisfied with his correct address, I allowed him to continue his journey, which he did, shouting more invective and swearing at me.

Several days later I was called to the office of our chief inspector where I was told that the West Indian man had made a formal complaint against me to Force Headquarters and had alleged that I had shown a bad racist attitude whereby I had been sitting at the side of the road waiting for a black man to harass. Also, that my language towards him had been disrespectful to his country and that I had made up the allegation regarding the white lines just to spite him.

The chief inspector advised me that, as there were two of them against my lone account, the best way out of the situation was to allow the summons to be waived. I refused but was over-ruled.

The West Indian did not even produce his documents. This was my first experience of racial hatred, but it was not white against black.

In this case it was "he who shouts the loudest wins the argument".

Back in the days of the 1960s, police cars were often called upon to pursue other cars for a number of reasons.

Some were as a result of a smash-and-grab or burglary but, as now, most were as a result of having been stolen. The stolen cars were mainly cheaper makes of Ford or Vauxhall and rarely matched the power of the traffic car and pursuits were quickly finished.

Most drivers merely crashed within a mile of the start of the chase. It seems that, today, the stolen cars are more powerful and the perpetrators have substantially more experience in handling them than was the case 40 years ago.

In the 1960s any perpetrator found guilty of stealing a car and trying to make off from pursuing police officers would, almost invariably, get a custodial sentence and a very long disqualification from driving. If they were then to be caught again, driving whilst disqualified, a further custodial spell would be applied.

The magistrates simply did not appreciate their decisions being ignored.

One of my most hair-raising chases involved a motorcycle rider and pillion passenger.

It was around midnight on the A20 at Farningham, near Brands Hatch motor racing circuit, when we decided to have a word with the riders of two motorcycles as they pulled into the Farningham petrol station.

As one motorcycle rider stopped by the fuel pumps, the other moved along the forecourt towards the far exit to wait for his colleague. As he stopped, the pillion rider turned round and saw our patrol car coming to rest behind them. He tapped his rider on the shoulder and away they went towards London.

We gave immediate pursuit but the motorcycle was a high powered model which drew away from us until we reached the Swanley by-pass, where we started to gain on our target.

At times, flames were visible from the exhaust pipes of the machine. Our speed peaked at nearly 120 mph.

My partner radioed to request our Ops Room to alert the Metropolitan Police that we were going to enter their jurisdiction and I attempted to keep up with the motorcycle.

After a few miles, we considered it prudent to call off the pursuit after the rider went through a set of traffic lights on red, actually passing between two cars that were crossing our path, whilst still in excess of 100 mph.

We understand that he was last seen by a Metropolitan patrol in Lewisham High Street with flames still belching from his exhaust pipes.

CHAPTER 13

Abominable Loads

THE TRAFFIC OFFICER of my era had many specialist duties that he was called on to perform. One of these was the escorting of abnormal loads (known colloquially as abominable loads) along the crowded Kentish roads. I often wondered why this was so necessary because such huge vehicles are very easy to see. It was the small vehicles that other drivers failed to see and had accidents with. However, most traffic men have tales to tell about escorting these behemoths of the road. Here are some of mine.

It was midnight at the top of Wrotham Hill on the old A20 which runs between Folkestone and London.

My colleague, Paul, and I had been told to escort a large load from the hilltop lay-by to Sidcup where it would again be laid up for the daylight hours and then taken onwards by the Metropolitan police escort the following night.

On arrival, we saw that it was an exceptionally large generator being operated by Pickfords Heavy Haulage in a "two pull one push" configuration. There were two heavy-load locomotive units at the front. These were Scammell 6X6 Constructor tractive units and were powered by Rolls Royce engines.

Their task was to provide the pulling factor for the huge, laden, trailer.

There was a similar unit at the back, attached to the trailer, for the purpose of providing a third means of propulsion as well as being equipped with the means of providing an effective braking effort, both by engine and braked wheels.

The whole combination weighed nearly 500 tons on countless wheels, and was nearly 150 feet in length. There was only one man in charge but he had about twelve other drivers and assistants.

Night time traffic was now very light and we got the escort underway. The speed was only 3-4 miles-per-hour so we soon became rather bored with leading this massive obstruction along such a wide, empty, unlit, road across the Kent countryside.

At about half past one we stopped near Brands Hatch motor racing circuit where we all piled into the leading tractor for a brew and to chat to the drivers and attendants about their work in taking these large loads all over the country.

The general consensus was that rarely did anything happen other than the demolishing of ill-placed Keep Left bollards, or the like.

Thus refreshed, we continued on in the total darkness of the A20 to descend the long hill known as Death Hill at Farningham—well named after the awful accident record of the hill ever since the road was first used by cars.

After only a few minutes of descending the hill, at approximately 2 miles-per-hour, I turned round in the passenger seat of the patrol car and noticed that the load was catching up with us. It was getting faster.

The speed increased to 5-6 miles-per-hour and smoke started to come from many of the wheels on the units.

Men were jumping out and grabbing large triangular blocks of timber and jamming them under the road-wheels, to little avail. The huge tyres just rose up over the wooden chocks and back down to the road surface with no apparent reduction in the speed of the unit.

The load was out of control!

The driver had even driven the nearside wheels up onto the grass verge in the hope that the soft ground would slow the runaway but, with little recent rain, the verge was as dry as the road surface and created no retarding effect at all.

Paul let me out and he drove on down Death Hill towards Farningham roundabout to erect signs—for what good they would do—and warn other traffic. I went back to the load and spoke to the head driver who told me that the rearmost unit had burned out its clutch and that the other two units were insufficient to apply enough braking on the descent. All would rest upon his men's efforts with the blocks.

As luck would have it, the next 100 yards or so was slightly less of a decline and, with everyone using the blocks, the load gradually slowed and finally stopped before the next steep section of road.

There was relief all round.

It was generally admitted that if the blocks had not worked, the load would have struck Farningham roundabout and the nearby filling station at a substantial speed and done enormous damage.

After letting the brakes cool down, which took well over an hour, the entire train was examined by the drivers and attendants until they were completely satisfied as to the integrity of the braking system. They then started the engines and the load was slowly moved to the next lay-by to receive further attention later that day.

Another memorable load was an extra-large caterpillar-tracked crane weighing about 75 tons, mounted on a low-loader trailer which was to be escorted from Swanscombe to south London.

The route was to be along the A2 past Dartford.

We checked the dimensions of the load against the details given on the load sheet to make sure that it was within the width and height permissible and then commenced our escort from Britannia Lead Works and brought it along the unmade road to the A226 to emerge by Gravesend football ground.

Whilst still travelling along the unmade road, the jib of the crane became caught up in low branches and pulled down a whole tree.

That took a good half-an-hour to remove and we resumed the drive along the trackway to come out onto the main road, then to turn right.

This particular bend on London Road, at the football ground, was super-elevated, meaning that the whole width of the road slanted down to the south. The northern edge of the road was therefore higher and created a crown over which the load must pass. Being a low-loader trailer, it bottomed-out on that crown and immediately became jammed. The tractive unit became stationary across the road at right-angles thus totally blocking a main commuter route –at 8o'clock in the morning.

It was chaos for almost an hour whilst the driver and his attendant acquired some steel rods and heavy-weight bottle jacks to raise the trailer, and roll it off the crown of the road by use of the steel rods which acted as the rollers.

Thus clear, we got a move on and drove up to the A2 where we made good speed towards London.

It was this speed which was to be our next mistake.

Recall the incident with the tree before we even got to the public road. Unbeknown to us, the jib of the crane had been knocked upwards some 10-12 inches when it struck the branches. No-one had thought it necessary to re-measure the height to ensure that it was still as notified. Now, instead of having a positive eight inches top clearance beneath the concrete footbridge across Princes Road at Dartford we had a negative two inches.

Because the jib was 10 inches higher than it should have been, the tip of the jib struck the concrete bridge at around 40 miles-per-hour.

The impact moved the entire bridge about 2 feet to the west on its supports, as well as wrecking the jib top, which fortunately folded up and slid underneath the concrete footbridge, having carved away a huge chunk of reinforced masonry from the underside of the span.

If the jib had been knocked any higher the force of the impact would probably have completely demolished the bridge, which would have fallen onto the trailer, crushing it.

The design of this type of footbridge is that they are held in place by the weight of the cross-section. There is no rigid fixing to maintain it in the erected position so as to allow for natural expansion and contraction in varying temperatures.

We had now effectively blocked the A2 which remained closed for several hours whilst we got engineers out to examine the damaged bridge. It was fortunate that we, as escorts, did not have to pay for these things, but what that load cost the nation that day is something about which I have speculated on with a smile.

All I know is that we did get our claimed overtime payment for being very late off duty.

A beautiful sunny day in the summer of 1968 saw us driving to the Metropolitan border to collect a large load, another 75 ton crane, bound for the Isle of Grain.

It was a very inconvenient time to receive these instructions because an important card game was scheduled to be held at Rochester police station canteen that lunchtime. Certain priorities are very important in the day-to-day life of traffic officers.

We met the driver for the briefing at Dartford Heath, telling him that we would travel ahead as far as the new dual carriageway at Gravesend, at which time we would allow him to pass us and then we would guard his rear-end on the dual carriageway. This was normal procedure when one police car was escorting an abnormal load.

My partner also explained to the lorry driver that we were not too concerned about *strictly* keeping to the abnormal-load speed limit (which was ridiculously low anyway, and held up other traffic) because we were already behind schedule.

We took up position ahead of the load and led it eastwards along the A2 through heavy two-way traffic. The lorry driver, although hauling a crane weighing some 75 tons (making a total road weight of some 90 tons on 10 axles), obviously had a powerful tractive unit and kept close to us at speeds nearing 40 miles-per-hour.

On reaching the start of the dual carriageway we moved to our nearside to allow the load to pass and duly fell in behind the trailer with our blue lights on to warn traffic catching us up that there was a wide, slow-moving vehicle ahead.

The A2 road immediately began a descent down the long hill of Swanscombe Cutting and the speed of the load increased; first to 50 miles-per-hour, then 60 miles-per-hour.

Next, the driver started to pass slower traffic, increasing speed even more.

He raced along the main road, being followed by the patrol car with lights ablaze, to the end of the dual carriage.

Only then did he allow us to re-pass him and we soon stopped the load to speak to the driver.

His excuse was that my partner had given him sanction to increase speed above the limit and he had taken us at our word. What he misunderstood was that we meant the speed limit for abnormal loads.

The bottom line was that we arrived for our lunch break at Rochester canteen in plenty of time to participate in the card game.

During the dark days of the 1960s police officers, in general, were tempted by the side benefits of providing their services. Pay rates remained at a low level for the hours worked and Police Regulations enforced the order that no police officer could take additional paid work, unlike professions such as the firemen, who regularly held down two, or sometimes more, jobs.

Being a police officer meant that several businesses offered appreciation for good work done by you in the form of money, or money's worth. Ejecting fighting customers in a Chinese restaurant may well lead to the offer of a free meal by the manager. A garage owner called out to an accident scene may offer a free or cut-price car service by way of thanks. One of the perquisites of escorting wide or heavy loads was that the transport managers of the haulage companies operating those abnormal loads frequently gave their drivers money to give to the police escorts in appreciation of their help.

We provided a prompt, professional service to the hauliers to help them complete their work efficiently and within time, for which they occasionally extended their gratitude. It was rarely a generous sum and such action in accepting it in these more modern times would probably be regarded as corrupt. Such reward was always presented freely and never asked for.

At midnight, one dark night, we had to attend at Dartford Heath to meet the Metropolitan police who were to pass a load on to us for its onward journey into Kent.

We were parked in the lay-by and the three motorcyclists from the Met escort group rode in behind our patrol car, having parked the load further back down the lay-by. The three escorting officers all squeezed into the back of our patrol car and cigarettes were handed out.

The sergeant in charge of the escort explained that the driver was going to have his break as he had just come right through central London without stopping.

Small talk continued, during which the subject of the perks was raised. The sergeant enquired as to whether we had any trouble getting the "dropsy", as the perquisites were called, from the drivers of this particular haulage company. I explained that it was not normal, to my knowledge, to receive any dropsy from this particular company, but it didn't concern us. The sergeant was incensed.

"Come with me," he said, and we all got out and followed him to the lorry cab where he dragged the driver out.

"I hear you don't "drop" these Kent lads," he said to the load driver, "How much does your transport manager give you to give to them?"

"Five pounds," was the reply.

The sergeant then gave the driver a severe lecture on honesty, based on the fact that the money was given by the haulage company to the driver, to pass on to us. The Met escorts always got theirs, so if the driver did not pass the allotted cash on to his Kent escort, he was obviously putting it into his own pocket, which was very dishonest and was stealing from his employer: even worse, it was constructive larceny from us, the police!

He then threatened the driver that if word came back to him that Kent traffic officers were NOT getting their rightful dropsy, he would ensure that other loads operated by the same haulier would sit up in north London for 24 hours and the drivers would be arrested for stealing the money.

It was then rather embarrassing to be told by the Metropolitan police sergeant that we should not encourage the haulier to be dishonest by not accepting the tip.

With that out of the way, we commenced our escort of the load and delivered it to the power station security gate where our responsibility ended.

We got out of the patrol car to speak with the driver and the site security staff, following which we returned to our car to find a fiver on the seat.

It would have been entirely wrong of us to hand it back to the driver because he certainly would not have given it back to his boss—and he earned a lot more than we did, anyway. What is a poor copper to do?

Then there was the wide load which we escorted along the old Rochester High Street in the early hours of the morning.

This thoroughfare is an ancient part of the original London to Dover road, since relieved by the M2 motorway further to the south but, in the 1960s, was a narrow shopping street lined with very old buildings of historic and architectural interest.

As we headed the load, there was a parked car on our left with the occupant sitting in the driver's seat and the engine running. His vehicle was in the general path of the approaching load so my colleague wound down the window to speak to the driver.

"Move over tight to your left. There is a wide load coming through," he said.

I moved off to get to the next junction and didn't actually see what happened next. I did see the aftermath and it was not very tidy.

Apparently, what happened was that the car driver looked in his mirror to see the approaching lorry with its lights full-on, and initially thought that there would be room for it to pass so he didn't move. He obviously couldn't see the additional nearside width of the load extending towards him.

The load driver had assessed that he could get through anyway and was going ahead at some 20 miles-per-hour. As the lorry cab passed the car-driver's position the driver panicked and decided to move over after all. He drove forward but failed to realise that his front wheels were inclined to the right, and the car immediately moved to the right before the driver could correct the angle, thus moving the car into the path of the huge caterpillar track of the crane on the low-loader. The track hit the rear offside corner of the car and spun it round to the left—straight into the protruding wall of a jeweller's shop.

The momentum of the lorry continued the pressure on the car, bending it, shortening it, and all the time, demolishing the wall of the jeweller's; and then the shop front window crashed out.

Alarms started ringing and Rochester High Street awoke! The report writing on that incident took many days.

Later in my service, I was to have a second posting on traffic division and the escorting of abnormal loads remained a task that was never free of incident.

CHAPTER 14

Another Change of Scenery

IN 1969 I decided that traffic division would have to do without me. I had attempted to become a traffic motorcyclist but that was a closed shop at Rochester, with a list of officers waiting for training. The routine of going out each day and booking people and clearing up their accidents was beginning to get me down, so I applied to return to the town to gain more experience in general police duties.

My wife and I, together with our two young daughters, were living in a police house at Rochester whilst I served at the traffic division and so it was convenient for me to merely transfer within the Medway Towns.

Chatham was to be my next posting, and I found that with seven years experience, I was one of the senior constables at this lively police station.

With that experience came some rewards and I was soon to become a station duty officer.

Being the station officer at a town station like Chatham was a very busy post. I was in the front office, manning the enquiry counter and maintaining the entries in the occurrence and crime books. I was in constant contact, via the new two-way personal radio system, with the other members of the section who were on patrol, and, most importantly, I had to make tea for the sergeant and the telephonist.

Chatham was certainly an extremely busy and, at that time, rather undermanned town. The volume of calls for assistance was frequently to strain the resources available, especially on Saturday nights.

One particular Saturday, all available patrols were dealing with serious incidents, traffic division had been called in to help and the late-turn officers were also doing overtime and trying to get off duty.

It was almost midnight and I answered yet another call for help which meant that I now had several serious incidents backed up with no-one available to attend them. The call was from the licensee of a public house just round the corner from the police station. I could hear the sound of smashing glass and screaming in the background. The caller requested immediate attendance of "lots of police".

I had to tell him that it was not possible and what was he doing with a pub full of drinkers at that hour anyway?

When I was, eventually, able to get our car there, everyone had gone home and the publican was beside himself with rage.

The station sergeant merely told him to write to his Member of Parliament, or stop serving alcohol at the lawful end of permitted hours.

One of the station sergeants to whom I was responsible was Sergeant Horton. Over thirty years in the job and never known to panic—ever.

The front office at Chatham was a place where panic should have been a daily event.

It was said that you should try and imagine the following scenario: a Boeing 747 airliner, fully laden with 400 passengers, is on its glide path over Kent towards Heathrow Airport and is known to have lost all power over the Medway Towns. It crashes down onto Luton arches, which is one of the busiest traffic junctions in the town and where the main London railway line passes over the road on a huge viaduct. A fully-laden passenger train is passing over the viaduct at the same time as the plane crashes on it. It is 8:30 in the morning and the rush hour is at its heaviest. The calls come flooding into the police station and Sergeant Horton is the recipient of the news of this dreadful catastrophe. It is said that his first words would probably be, "Who is on Seven Beat this morning?"

Among the legends surrounding him, I have first knowledge of a memorable event which occurred one evening at the front office.

For a change, it was a very quiet evening and I was seated in the telephone corner, idling time away with a cup of tea and a coffee-cream biscuit. Sergeant Horton was standing, leaning forward, at the hatchway shelf that gave head and shoulders access to public callers, writing a slow but methodically correct entry into the occurrence book in his inimitable copperplate handwriting.

We had heard, but hadn't particularly commented upon, a sound like a car back-firing somewhere in the general vicinity.

Suddenly the public door of the police station burst open and a young man staggered across the hallway towards the hatchway, saw Sergeant Horton and shouted, "I've been shot. I've been shot!!!"

It was then that I realised it had not been the sound of a backfire from a car, but a gunshot.

Sergeant Horton did not even look up. He merely told the man, tersely, not to interrupt and to go and sit down on the seat. The amazed man did as he was told and Sergeant Horton asked me to pass him the ruler, which I did.

He then slowly, and in great detail, concluded his entry in the book, signed his name and rank, then double-underlined his writing.

He put down the pen and ruler and closed the book.

He placed it under the counter in its appropriate home and then gazed out to the seat where the man was slumped in a spreading pool of dark red blood.

"Now, young man," he said, "where have you been shot?"

On seeing the amount of blood going all over the public entrance floor, we felt morally obliged to go to the injured man to elicit some detail from him.

It turned out that he had a clean wound where a bullet had obviously passed through the fleshy part of his upper leg, leaving rather a messy exit area.

Basic aid was given from the rather less than extensive First Aid box in the front office and the flow of blood was controlled. Although there was lots of blood, Sergeant Horton did not think that the artery had been affected so he called in a Panda car to take the man to hospital, and to obtain a statement from him.

I had the temerity to enquire if we shouldn't, perhaps, do something about the man who had fired the shot, wherever he was.

Silly me! Sergeant Horton gave me his theory that, a) the assailant would not be hanging about after shooting a man in such proximity to a police station so it would be pointless to get all four of the late turn officers involved in a manhunt, or, b) If the man were to be so stupid as to hang around, that would mean that he was mad as well as armed and, therefore, we should assume that he was dangerous. It would be silly to go out there just yet without a firearms officer being present.

Common sense really.

He then telephoned headquarters to speak to the operations room duty officer and advise him to call out the firearms team to attend at Chatham where we would have some information when they arrived.

When I say "Firearms Team" I use the term advisedly. In 1969 armed police officers were virtually unknown.

Arms were available to Special Branch officers and some weapons were available from the police station safe, but no-one interfered with the personal off-duty life of our superintendent, who was the only one with a key and the ability to give permission for its use.

The injured man was able to tell the constable who took him to hospital who had pulled the trigger, and why.

Consequently, it transpired that the gunman had immediately boarded a train from Chatham to London, where he lived. Four days later, he was shot by the Metropolitan Police (who had a lot more guns than Kent officers) whilst resisting arrest at a stand-off on a council estate.

That proved to all of us that Sergeant Horton's actions had been entirely correct and safeguarded the manpower, not to say the good health of our late-turn officers until another day.

Public order in Chatham was frequently a problem for police. In those days Chatham was still a major naval town, as it had been for many hundreds of years.

It contains one of the best-preserved ship-building facilities in the world, with a history of military ship-building of over 400 years, originally using Kentish oaks.

The entrance to the River Medway had been developed, around the shipyard, as huge dock areas which enabled quite large warships to tie up.

There was a major shore-based Royal Naval establishment, HMS Pembroke, which was permanently manned.

Navy ships from around the world visited the dockyard, both as courtesy visits and for re-stocking and repair. The consequence was that ratings from the ships would be able to have a run ashore to enjoy the wondrous delights of Chatham night life. (For readers not familiar with the town of Chatham, that was a rather weak joke).

It was said that one hundred years ago there were well over 100 premises selling ale along the length of Rochester and Chatham High Streets. That figure is well reduced since those heady days but on run-ashore nights the remaining public houses did a roaring trade.

The town hall clock striking 11 o'clock at night brought out all of our problems at once.

Rarely would Chatham town be able to put out more than four foot-officers onto the High Street area on an average night duty. That was clearly insufficient to deal with any fights or other squabbles which might break out between naval ratings and local troublemakers.

Sometimes there was inter-ship rivalry if more than two crews were on shore at the same time.

Fortunately, the navy have a unit called the Naval Patrol. This is a group of naval regulating officers who have a team of, generally, rather large seamen who are charged with discipline on board ship, and within a certain radius of the port when on shore.

The Naval Patrol had some very long and very hard nightsticks, with which they coaxed the most unwilling sailor from his lamppost. It was always a very reassuring sight to see the patrol van coming down the street just as mass brawling was going on. Even our own local hooligans were in awe of the heavy stick and it did them no good to complain the next day.

Chatham Town Police and HMS Pembroke always maintained a very good social relationship, leading to some very enjoyable evenings for our families.

As a shore establishment, Pembroke maintained a training school for naval chefs and it was a regular thing for the superintendent to get an invite for up to twenty police officer and their wives to attend a soiree at the base. The evening was semi-formal and started with a welcome from the Naval Commander in the main ballroom.

To start the proceedings a traditional measure of grog would be served to everyone as they came into the building and the naval band would play background music, as well as provide entertainment for dancing.

The rest of the evening would be spent mixing with the officers and their ladies and then to be seated and served by the students and ratings with the most tasty food.

It should be mentioned that the tradition of taking a drink of rum in the Royal Navy (splicing the mainbrace) had been enjoyed since 1687 and all came to an end on 31st July 1970 when, sadly, the tradition finished. Navy rum was a very thick spirit which was watered down by adding a quart of water to a pint of rum. The result was grog, hence the saying, "to get groggy". I understand that the Royal Navy still "splice the mainbrace" for notable events such as Royal Weddings and the like, but it is now done with beer.

The bar at these Naval soirees was one of those popular cheap bars, subsidised by a local brewery, and led to the absolute necessity of transport home.

Usually it was in the regulator's van but, occasionally, in the prison van from the police station.

Even rarer, if you were very unlucky, you would have to obtain a local taxi and actually pay for the privilege of being taken home. But they were always memorable nights.

Within Chatham Naval Base was the nuclear submarine facility which was used for the servicing of our Polaris fleet of submarines.

The other major base with a similar reason for existence was at Faslane on the River Clyde near Glasgow.

Many years before, commencing in 1907, many standard submarines had been constructed and launched from Chatham Dockyard but this work had been reduced in the 1960s with the last one, HM Submarine Okanagan, being launched in 1968.

Money had then been spent on creating the nuclear facility. This facility was top secret and well-guarded by naval personnel, all subject to the Official Secrets Act.

One day, I found myself in possession of a report from Lanarkshire Police which required me to interview a naval rating who had fallen foul of the Scottish Police in respect of his vehicle documentation, or lack of it.

He was based on the nuclear submarine, HM Submarine Valiant, which had arrived in dry dock at Chatham preparatory to undergoing a major re-fit. The crew were still based on board but were able to visit the town and generally leave the facility when their duty allowed. All, it seemed, other than this particular rating.

He had fallen foul of naval discipline and was confined to ship so I made an application through the regulator's office to interview him in the regulating officer's room near the dockyard gate.

On the appointed day, I turned up to be told that his commanding officer did not even want him leaving Valiant and that, subject to passes, I should interview him on-board the vessel.

I was given a pass into the dockyard where I made my way, with a note of the appointment, to the Nuclear Submarine facility. It required a separate pass to enter that compound.

I was finally allowed in and made my way to the dry dock, where I found yet another pass was needed to get through a metal barrier to actually get on board. That was duly issued after more telephone calls.

Whilst waiting at the barrier, I was astonished by the size of this nuclear submarine, only having seen pictures of submarines from the last world war. Its dimensions were truly enormous.

A rating appeared and took me on board, or rather through a hole in the deck. I duly followed the rating down steps, along passages, up steps, round corners, until I reached an office where my subject was seated at a table, along with a junior officer who had to be present under these circumstances.

I conducted the formal interview and reported the sailor for his Scottish indiscretions, following which he requested time to have an informal conversation with me about the best way for him to deal with his problem. The junior officer then excused himself as he no longer felt his need to be present.

After a few more minutes chat, the loudspeakers came on and ordered the rating to a particular venue at once. So he left, leaving me alone in the bowels of a totally strange nuclear submarine in which I got hopelessly lost.

Never mind, I would be able to find my own way out without too much of a problem.

After about five minutes of getting even more lost, I found myself confronted by quite a senior naval officer with two plums in his mouth. He was obviously very surprised to encounter a civilian police constable in full uniform walking along the corridor of his nuclear submarine.

"What are you doing down here?" He demanded.

"I am trying to get to Woolworths, in Chatham High Street. Perhaps you could direct me, sir?" I replied.

He failed to see the funny side of my quip and I was quickly escorted out of the submarine by a rating. This rating said to me, in a low voice, "You do know you found your way up to the dodgy end, don't you?"

What he actually meant by that, I didn't know, but I have lived to tell the tale.

CHAPTER 15

Crime Reporting in the Medway Towns

THE CRIME RATE in the Medway Towns, comprising Rochester, Chatham, Gillingham and Rainham was the highest per capita in Kent. Chatham topped the figures for the Medway Towns. Simply, there were not enough police officers to deal with the volume of calls and crime complaints. The CID sections were always under severe pressure to maintain an acceptable "clear-up" rate and steps were taken to ensure that figures were somehow kept in check.

One Saturday, there were an unusual number of reports made to the front office concerning lost purses.

The quandary that the station officer found himself in was, should he enter the lost purses individually in the lost property book or should he assume that there was a purse-snatcher at large who was responsible for all these losses.

The detective inspector in charge of local figures did not like uniformed constables assuming that 15 lost purses from the High Street in a two-hour period was anything but carelessness on the part of their owners and insisted on the lost-property book route being taken.

Then, when the purse-snatcher was eventually caught, he could be charged with every purse lost in the town since the previous Easter holiday, and all those listed crimes were solved in one fell swoop. This was something to do with massaging crime reporting figures for the superintendent.

These stealers of purses operated in many of the town centres and their effectiveness could be assumed by the number of lost-property book entries made by cowering station officers, scared of the wrath of the detective inspector.

If politicians had known of the way that crime statistics were massaged at the whim of certain senior officers, perhaps they would not have given them so much credibility.

It has always been the understanding amongst working police officers that if a motor-crime unit is launched, then motor-crime figures will increase (both reported and solved).

The same goes with drug units. A town without a drug unit does not have an obvious problem with drugs. Launch a drugs unit, and the respective figures will reveal a totally different story.

CHAPTER 16

Looking to Move On

AFTER A YEAR or so at Chatham, which, I have to say, was a short but enjoyable time with plenty of variety, I chose to apply for a place on the Dog Section. Each division had at least two dog handlers allocated to the strength, even though they were under the control of Force HQ at Maidstone. My positive attitude to their work had been recognised by the existing members, which was a very important plus point in becoming a dog handler as it was a very close-knit unit with a good camaraderie. I had been interviewed by the senior officer in charge of police dogs at Headquarters and told that I would be strongly considered for either Gravesend or Sevenoaks as soon as the vacancy arose. I had spoken at some length with my wife to make sure that she was fully aware of the dedication that we would both have to put into such a change of direction. She was happy with my arguments and agreed that she was fully prepared for the increased responsibility of having a new, four-legged member of the family to join our two young daughters. The thought of having to move house and live in a town like Gravesend was not immediately appealing and I could only hope that a posting to the better-regarded town of Sevenoaks would be the first choice. With this happy thought in mind, on a cold day in early February 1970, we put all our immediate concerns behind us and travelled by car to London on a rare day out to visit the annual Boat Show at Earls Court. Not that I had any desire to become a master mariner of any sort; the chance of a day trip to the exhibition just seemed attractive at the time.

On our return later that evening, I found the duty inspector from Chatham sitting in his car outside my house. As I put my car into the garage, he got out of his police car and stood waiting to speak to me which I considered to be rather ominous.

I asked him in and enquired if there was a problem. He commented upon my application to join the dog section and asked if I would like to persevere with that change of direction, OR, did I want to be rural policeman?

This news came like a bolt out of the blue. I asked where the posting would be to and he replied, "It's the other end of the county. A small village called Elham".

It transpired that the current incumbent had misbehaved and was to receive a "punishment" posting to Chatham and somebody from Chatham was going to be exchanged to take the place at Elham. It was to be a straight swop and take place within two weeks.

I gave the inspector a cup of tea whilst I discussed the decision with my wife and, after a very few seconds, decided that my Dog Section application would be put on the back burner and that the future would be a move to east Kent to be a village bobby.

I later had to make a very humble approach to my colleagues in the Dog Section and explain why I had taken the decision not to join their brethren and plead what a difficult decision it had been.

As I mentioned earlier, East Kent was my family home before my commitment to becoming a police officer and receiving a posting to the western end of this lovely county. I recalled happy memories of my early days when my mother and father had driven me through the winding country lanes, sometimes ending up at Elham which, to me, was one of the most charming villages in Kent; very typical of the county.

So it was that two weeks later we packed up the furniture, the cat and our two daughters and moved to the Police House at Elham where we were to spend several happy years.

The family isolation in West Kent was to become a thing of the past. In retrospect, those eight years spent between Dartford and the Medway Towns had caused a loss of regular contact with family and friends of my pre-police days.

Although within the same county, it was always half a day's travel to get home and police pay in those days did not allow for the additional expense of travel. The duty of working three weekends out of four also made visiting old friends very difficult and I saw the move to East Kent as a chance to see a lot more of our extended families in the future.

CHAPTER 17

Life as a Village Bobby

NUMBER 2, POLICE House, Elham, was located on the south side of Elham in an elevated position, surrounded by towering trees, and next to the Elham Church of England Primary School. In fact, my daughters were the only pupils who did not have to cross any road to get to school. I merely lifted them over the chain link fence for them to walk across the playing field to the schoolroom. To the east was a wonderful view across the Elham Valley over a large garden for vegetables, flowers and for the girls to play. I considered that this would be a very pleasant location to live and I was not to be disappointed.

My neighbour at 1, Police House was another officer with a young family.

These were two adjoining police houses, connected by the police office in the middle and, together, he and I would have responsibility for the parish of Elham, and further shared duties with several other officers in neighbouring villages covering a large rural swathe of south-east Kent with a rural headquarters office at Hythe police station.

It was one of the largest rural sub-divisions in the county by area, being almost 20 miles from north to south.

Our home was not supplied with mains gas and my new colleague suggested that we consider an alternative method to electric heating, central heating not having been adopted in older homes. There was a coke boiler in the kitchen and an open coal/wood hearth in the sitting room but, with no other heating, the upstairs rooms, in particular, were difficult to keep warm for the children.

His warnings were heeded that week, and not a moment too soon.

In the centre of the village were half a dozen retail premises that, for a great many years, had been vital to the villagers, many of whom had no transport to get to the larger towns.

These premises included a general provisions store, a butchers shop, and a wonderful bakers shop with the old bakery at the back which always produced that wonderful smell so reminiscent of freshly-baked bread.

There was a small local garage with two petrol pumps and attended service but, most important, was the ironmonger, Mr Bain.

His single-fronted shop on the High Street was bigger inside than it was outside! Packed to the rafters with every sort of item that a major Do-it-Yourself store now provides, he sold materials for building, carpentry, gardening and other household goods—including paraffin heaters and fuel. It really was an essential shop but the likes of the giant B&Q stores have now mostly removed such useful shops from the face of the earth. Anyway, my new paraffin heater came from there.

Within a few days of moving to Elham in that winter of 1970, the weather forecast was for rain, turning to snow. What an accurate forecast that turned out to be.

We awoke to find heavy rain falling.

This rain turned to sleet by mid-morning, then to heavy snow by noon. There was little wind blowing and the snow settled readily as the air temperature became colder.

By mid afternoon, all traffic through the village, which was a main route between Folkestone and Canterbury, had stopped.

By 5pm, it was dark and the electric power to the whole village failed. Other villages were also plunged into outages caused by the weight of snow building up on overhead power lines that served these rural communities.

Still the snow continued to fall exceptionally heavily. It finally ceased at 7pm, leaving the entire village in an eerie light with the new snow covering everything in sight.

All was totally silent with bright starlight and it became increasingly cold as the temperature plunged to well below zero.

We had prepared an evening meal for the girls and, with no television or houselights, lit the nightlights and put the new paraffin heater in their bedroom.

My neighbour kindly offered to watch over them so that my wife and I could explore the village and find the local pub. The girls were quite happy to see us go as they were more excited to see the thick carpet of snow.

The combination of the clear rural atmosphere and lack of any light pollution meant that the moonless night allowed millions of stars to be visible which provided a soft light that enhanced the scene outside.

Diane and I dressed up in thick coats and rubber boots and trudged through nearly 18 inches of virgin snow to the village pub, a route that took us across the medieval square with its half-timbered homes all covered and surrounded by deep snow.

The only light was from oil lamps and candles in the windows of the homes, reflecting in the pure white snow that covered everything.

We reached the old King's Head public house in Elham Square and entered into a lovely warm fug. The open fire was alive with blazing logs and there were ancient oil lamps burning on the bar, illuminating the public area.

What a way to try out our "local" for the very first time. With everyone in the same situation, the locals proved to be a very agreeable group of villagers and we were able to form early friendships in this wonderful atmosphere.

The following day I was on duty, and spent it around the village as transport did not start running again until well into the day.

The main road did not open to traffic until the afternoon, although many of the minor roads had been opened up by local farmers. I was to find that, in the country, the old customs of neighbourly help and co-operation were still very much alive.

Most farmers had snowblade attachments for their tractors and were only too willing to extend snow clearance from their immediate roadways to the greater length of lanes within the parish, thus allowing essential services to access outlying homes more easily.

During those early snowy days I patrolled around the village meeting the residents and giving help to elderly villagers whose presence was indicated to me. Such minor tasks as getting logs in and ensuring that people were comfortable led to good relationships that were to last for my duration in Elham.

Such was the severity of this winter blast that the nearby village of Stelling Minnis was without any electricity for eight days, the blizzard having brought down far more power lines than the emergency linesmen could cope with.

Much of this damage had occurred in outlying areas that were, in those conditions, impossible to reach even with specialist vehicles.

For several days we local rural officers remained mostly in our villages continuing to give assistance to those who needed it, and it gave me plenty of time to study local information regarding the surrounding area and the identity of distant householders who might need attention—good and bad.

My only official transport was a motorcycle which was completely useless in any sort of snow or ice; so that stayed in my garage.

The rural section, which comprised of some ten officers in neighbouring villages, shared the use of an emergency response vehicle in which we undertook 999 duties on a rota basis.

During the snowy weather it was handed over to the next officer on shift who returned the previous driver to his home. However, the usual process in normal weather was to ride the motorcycle to Hythe police station for a changeover at the rural office.

The motorcycle allocated to me was an ancient Velocette Li 150 that had already completed well over 30,000 miles—well beyond the usual mileage normally expected of such a small capacity machine. Consequently, it lacked power and, like my old Velocette at Dartford several years earlier, caused many embarrassing moments.

Elham is a particularly hilly area, set as it is in a pleasant chalkland valley with steep, narrow roads.

Frequently, it was necessary to dismount and walk alongside the machine with the engine running in first gear because it did not have the power to carry me up the hill. Not that I was overweight; it just couldn't cope.

The ignominy of being passed by one of my local, smiling parishioners whilst I was pushing the motorcycle up a steep incline remains fresh in my mind.

Our allocated emergency car was not much better. It was a Hillman Imp saloon with an aluminium 875cc engine mounted at the rear. Generally, it was a fairly unreliable vehicle with a tendency for the gearstick to become detached at the wrong moment.

Another serious problem was that it only had two doors, so the conveyance of prisoners who chose not to get into the car for whatever reason—mostly alcoholic—was nigh on impossible. It simply was too small.

During the early 1970s, because of world events, fuel supply to the UK became a national problem and we were told to do our bit and reduce our daily mileage as much as we could.

Orders came down from Headquarters that a shift (8 hours) mileage allowance of 40 miles should be applied.

The demands of rural policing against urban policing usually meant that far longer journeys were necessary to get between incidents and other duty commitments, yet we seemed to be given the same shift mileage allowances as the town cars from Folkestone and Hythe.

As I mentioned earlier, it was almost 20 miles from one end of the "patch" to the other, so one return trip used up that allowance.

What were we to do for the other seven hours?

My colleagues were concerned that they would be in trouble with the inspector if they constantly exceeded the mileage allowed so I suggested an answer from my existing traffic division knowledge of the Hillman Imp.

The speedometer cable entered the back of the dashboard via a screw joint. It was possible to reach behind the display panel, unscrew the retaining sleeve and detach the cable from the drive within the speedometer head, therefore stopping the odometer from recording the true mileage, when excessive daily travel was expected to occur.

After all, we were an emergency vehicle and if a 999 call was to be answered then the distance had to be covered.

Providing that the shift mileage was OK, the use of petrol was never questioned as it was automatically assumed that the small cars would be economical. The car manufacturer quoted a consumption rate of some 35-45 miles-per-gallon.

It appeared that on some days, our consumption appeared to fall to 15-20 miles-per-gallon—sometimes worse than that—but it was never picked up by the office staff, and the police work got done.

That is one of the unforeseen advantages of having separate administration departments. One does mileage reports whilst the other does petrol returns and never the two do meet!

It did not take long for me to realise that rural policing was certainly "policing by consent", as opposed to the method of policing practised in the more urban areas of West Kent.

Dealing with some face-to-face problems in the rural area of south-east Kent meant that the officer had to use significant diplomacy in his immediate actions because the time taken for any reinforcements to arrive at the scene could be anything up to twenty minutes.

Many times I encountered situations where, in a town, help would be forthcoming in a couple of minutes, but consideration had to be taken in rural situations, when faced with possible hostility or violence, that assistance could be a long time in coming.

One quiet Sunday afternoon I attended a call to Hawkinge village following a reported disturbance in a residential cul-de-sac.

On arrival I found that the adult son of one of the residents had thrown a television through a neighbour's front window and was now trying to fight everyone who approached him. The son had a long history of severe mental illness and I had knowledge of his violent background.

The local village bobby, who had been off duty that weekend, then appeared on the scene and, between the two of us, we managed to overpower the well-built young man after several minutes of strenuous effort and some loss of blood.

With Bill and I holding the man in what is colloquially known in wrestling circles as the Folding Body Press, we called to an onlooker to request a car from Folkestone police station, some five miles away, to come to our aid and help take the man to the cells. We were informed that Folkestone police station was sending a car immediately.

We waited—and waited. An hour passed! All of the time we were holding the young man, bent double, in the gutter of the roadway. Bill was holding one arm and kneeling on one leg, whilst I was doing the same on the man's other side. Only in that way could he be kept under our control and we remain relatively safe.

We had to ease the force being exerted from time to time to save him from passing out, but whenever we released our hold slightly he became violent again.

Our situation was becoming desperate and both of us were extremely fatigued.

We asked the onlooker to try to contact the police station again and see what was delaying the assistance that we so urgently required and, after the call was made, he came over and told us that the police car had been involved in an accident *en route* to us and that they were trying to find another car—but it was Sunday and we might have to wait a bit longer.

Eventually, a traffic division car arrived and the man was taken to the police station from where he was admitted to a mental hospital under the Mental Health Act.

A week later, he escaped and hanged himself from a railway bridge in front of a passing train.

I was just pleased that Bill, who had been spending a quiet afternoon with his feet up watching the football, was good enough to turn out and help me in his village.

This was also a good example of the camaraderie amongst rural policemen.

I was also to find that in the villages, the country folk are far more willing to assist the lone officer in a problematical situation than urban folk. Whilst at Elham, I was to find that the regular constabulary was augmented by excellent "Specials".

The local Special Constabulary officers consisted of an inspector, a sergeant and three constables, all resident in the village and available for duties at local events, mostly under the direction of the village policeman.

By normal occupation, they were all locally employed and mostly middle-aged (or more). One was the driver of the local effluent tanker normally engaged in emptying residents' cess pits. One was a butcher at the local shop. Another was a jeweller and the others were in agricultural work.

They were a fine team and were well-respected residents within the community, unlike other Specials from the towns, who seemed to think they were rather important and frequently dealt with the public in a disrespectful way.

My Specials were always willing to turn out to help police rural events such as gymkhanas, hunt meetings, country fetes, and fairs, where the additional arrival of townspeople caused congestion and possible disorder some way beyond that normally experienced in our small villages.

CHAPTER 18

Elham Life

IT WOULD SEEM to be good sense to take an interest in the area in which you live. City dwellers relate to the sights and sounds of urban life. The convenience of living in an urban area could be said to be enhanced by the relationship with that environment, shopping outlets, cinemas, bus services, together with the hustle and bustle of traffic, office buildings, and the general activities accessible to townsfolk. The countryside, to most urban dwellers, is where the woodland lies and where rural pastures are full of sheep and cows. Many better-off city types choose to live in the country whilst working in the city, and often take less heed of country ways or simply fail to understand the quieter way of life.

Country people who were brought up to the rural way of life, mostly appreciate the fresh air, dark nights, a proximity to animals, both domestic and wild, and value living closer to nature than the urban resident.

Country life is simply quieter, slower and steeped in the sort of traditions that are not experienced or easily understood by urban dwellers.

My family, their parents and their ancestors were all from rural east Kent, brought up to the country life, and I was pleased to be posted to a rural area that was unspoiled by the urban spread so prevalent in this part of England.

Within the village were several families who could trace their lineage back centuries.

Traditions were strong and the villagers were proud of their way of life. Of course there were newcomers but, for the most part, they joined with the local folk to enjoy life in this picturesque valley.

One of the advantages of having newcomers was that they were, generally, people of substance. Professional people who had good jobs in the towns. Men who had gone to good schools where they played cricket. Elham desperately needed young men who could play cricket!

The Elham Cricket Club had been established for well over a hundred years and played their matches on the village sports ground to the north of the village.

A local farmer had donated the land many years earlier, so it was rent-free and maintained by a small group of local enthusiasts that were typical in this area of rural life.

The ground was a triangular field with a beautifully kept square upon which the wickets were marked. There was a small pavilion clad with cedar tiles that was barely large enough for the two teams to assemble and prepare for the game.

On my arrival in the village I had decided to get involved with local leisure activities and, as a medium quality cricketer, had applied to join the Elham Valley Cricket Team with a view to playing for them as well as participating in the club activities of pitch preparation, and associated work like sweeping the pavilion and making sandwiches. I joined the committee and eventually became vice-chairman of the club.

During the summer seasons I spent many hours on the grass, preparing wickets and maintaining the outfield so that fair games of cricket could be played.

One of the areas that I could assist with was the acquisition of items of machinery necessary for the club to keep a good ground.

In the course of my travels around the area, dealing with police matters, I frequently came upon information that would lead to financially advantageous purchases such as a new set of gang-mowers for the outfield or a heavy roller for the wicket.

One day the committee revealed that our old tractor had finally expired and a new tractor (or, should I be clear, a better second-hand tractor) was urgently needed. By luck, I was aware that an original grey Ferguson TE20 tractor had became available after the passing of a Barham farmer a few weeks earlier.

It was going to be entered into a farm sale but I spoke to the widow, who was known to me through previous police work, and she agreed to let the club have it, providing they could get it going and transport it the three miles to our ground.

Several of the committee, complete with tools and fuel, came with me to the farm and, after some effort, we managed to get the engine going. After all, the old grey Fergy, as it is still affectionately known, was built between 1946 and 1956 and this particular model was one of the early ones.

The farmer's wife then revealed to us that the tractor had not been used for some fifteen years and she didn't think it would ever start again.

Some air was pumped into the tyres and I escorted the tractor through the back lanes to the cricket ground, escorted by my police van with a blue light going, just to make sure that it got there without incident (and insurance and tax) to begin work pulling the gang mowers.

As well as inter-village and league matches, the cricket club got involved in some great charity matches.

One of the most memorable was organised by a London medical consultant who had a holiday home in Elham and did occasionally turn out for us. He was a very good bowler and once had a trial for a minor county before getting serious about routing about in people's bodies.

He decided to organise a match between his colleagues in a London hospital and our country fellows, to take place at both home and away venues.

The home match was held on our picturesque ground at Elham, together with tea during the interval and a pub session in the evening. It was very successful, especially so, as we won.

The return match entailed a coach trip to Holland Park in north London one sunny Sunday.

Regrettably, several of our better players could not attend so we had to press-gang some locals into coming with us to make up numbers.

We travelled by hired coach to north London and had lunch with the surgeon at his home, which was very nice. He plied us with quantities of alcoholic beverage and we were too naive to appreciate the consequences of his generosity.

We then adjourned to the ground in a very relaxed condition and were amazed to see Holland Park cricket pitch surrounded by several rows of deck chairs and an audience of several hundred Londoners who had been told that a Kent side would be playing.

I believe many thought that the Kent County Cricket club were coming, but they were disappointed as four of our team didn't even have "whites".

The game commenced and we realised that the other team were really taking it seriously with several young players showing extreme quality.

We did field a couple of good bowlers and managed to bowl them out for a reasonable score but with most of us suffering from the lunchtime spent imbibing, I fear that we were not showing our best efforts.

Our batting reply was becoming dismal and we were heading for humiliation when in walked our number 10, a very portly, and slightly inebriated, shepherd called Arthur who was bereft of whites or cricket boots.

He sauntered to the wicket with his bat over his shoulder, an unbuttoned grey cardigan showing his fine girth and a broad smile on his weather-beaten face. He then swung the blade with such abandon that he won the match in short order whilst hitting several balls into the long grass some distance from the playing area.

Arthur was simply phenomenal and received the loudest cheer of the day as the disappointed team of doctors patted him on the back on his way to the pavilion—and more drink. Being involved in such events, for a local police officer, was a privilege.

Within the parish of Elham I could count some forty farms or homesteads that relied on agricultural produce to make a living. These varied in size between the extensive farmland owned by the major landowners to the smallholdings which relied upon a few animals or orchards to provide a livelihood.

One of the early priorities of the rural policeman is to call on these folk and get to know them because their knowledge of the area and local people was an important resource.

Most landowners had firearms or shotguns for the control of vermin and, accordingly, there was always the opportunity to chat whilst dealing with their regular renewals of firearm and shotgun certificates.

A couple of the older residents still applied for what was known as a "black powder licence" which entitled them to fill their own cartridges. Black powder is a highly explosive mixture of saltpetre, charcoal and sulphur and is mixed together in specific amounts to make basic gunpowder.

This was a lot cheaper than buying 8-bore or 12-bore shot cartridges from the gunsmith but did have an attendant danger that had to be acknowledged.

One particular smallholder, who was of advanced years but still had the hearing and sight of a wild animal, was one such resident whom I had to visit regarding his black powder licence renewal.

It was a cold winter's day when I called at his tiny cottage at the back of beyond. He welcomed me in, sat me down in the parlour in front of a spitting chestnut-wood, open fire and handed me a chipped mug containing a measure of his home-made cider. He then asked me to complete the form for him (he was never academically adept) whilst he got on with his work.

On a low table in front of the fire was the simple apparatus for the preparation of loading blank cartridges with shot and black powder, which he continued to do whilst chatting to me.

"Do you always load up the black powder like that?" I asked.

"My father taught me how over 60 years ago, sonny".

"What about the danger from the open hearth?" I asked.

"Never had an accident yet", he said, grinning at me.

Whilst I was sure that what he was doing was highly dangerous—not least to me, actually being present for this work—I did not feel qualified to offer criticism to such an expert in his labour. I merely completed the paperwork, finished the measure of delicious scrumpy and took my leave.

On the way out he handed me a bundle in a wrap of newspaper and said "I take it you know how to skin and cook a rabbit?" I didn't, but I do now.

The advantages of police officers dealing with the request for renewals of Firearms and Shotgun Certificates were that it gave the opportunity to visit people in their homes and get to know them better.

At the opposite end of the scale to my black powder friend was the retired Major-General of the British Army who had reached advanced years after a lifetime service, including a distinguished wartime record.

Being a retired officer of notable rank he had retained the custom of continuing to be known as "Major-General" and was afforded due respect by all who were aware of his background.

He had recently moved from another county into a small bungalow in the village and, although I had been aware of his position and residency in the village, I had never yet had cause to speak with him.

Into my "In Tray" one day came a Firearms Certificate renewal notice relating to a Part One Firearm under the control of this retired gentleman, so I telephoned him and made arrangements to call upon him in order to complete the necessary paperwork.

The following day I called at the bungalow and was welcomed by a tall, distinguished but casually dressed man who invited me in and offered refreshment. I immediately found him to be an amazing character and we chatted for some time about his experiences, leading to the history of the firearm that was subject of this renewal.

It appears that it was a German Luger pistol that had been Field Marshall Rommel's sidearm in Africa. As such, it was a trophy of war and was now permanently displayed in a regimental museum in Hampshire, although remaining the property of my applicant.

The original Firearm Certificate had been granted by the Chief Constable of Hampshire several years earlier, even though, strictly speaking, the term "trophy of war" did not relate to World War II, but to World War I and earlier. Obviously there was no intent to use the pistol and, as it was in a military museum for the duration, the security of it was totally satisfactory. I completed the forms and collected the fee due, informing the gentleman that his certificate would be sent to him in due course.

A few days later I was called to the inspector's office at Folkestone police station where the duty inspector gave me a telling-off for ignoring the rules regarding a trophy of war.

He suggested that I go back to the retired Major General, (whom he regarded as a plain "Mr" as he was now out of the army) and kindly inform him that the Kent Police do not renew illegal certificates—even for people like him—and that he should relinquish any claim to the gun, even if it was special to him.

On my return to the village later that day, I telephoned the Major General to request a further conversation regarding the renewal application and he invited me back to his home where he insisted that we partook of a small drink.

I explained that it was my senior officer's stance—not mine—that, even though the weapon was of extreme personal interest, it was the official view of the Kent Police that any possession of a World War II weapon was illegal and that he would have to relinquish his Firearms Certificate and, probably, donate the gun permanently to the regimental museum.

On receiving that information, he gave long consideration to what I had explained.

"Do you have the number of your Chief Constable's office at Maidstone, please?" he asked.

I provided him with the number and he, in my presence, telephoned the CC's secretary and, on identifying himself, spoke to the head of Kent Police, explaining the dilemma.

It was also obvious by the first names being used between them that they were known to each other. On conclusion of the call, he told me that matters had been resolved and that the certificate would be renewed.

Common sense had prevailed and when my path next crossed with the duty inspector at Folkestone police station, he intimated that we were not friends anymore.

When I first arrived at Elham I sat down with my more experienced neighbour who outlined the priorities for maintaining a happy life as a village bobby. "Get to know the important people", he said. (My retired Major General was one of them).

He then named half a dozen local people with whom it would be advantageous to have a working relationship. Among these was the local huntsman who was primarily in charge of the day-to-day administration of the East Kent Hunt, which was located on the western edge of the village not far from the police houses.

The hunt, known locally as the Elham Valley Hunt, occupied premises and land that included a large stable block, kennels, open fields and the huntsman's cottage, which was really a detached house where the huntsman lived with his family.

I had always held a rather ambivalent view where hunting was concerned but tended towards support because of the country tradition.

I recalled, as a child, watching the hunt in the village where I lived and was in awe of those large men in red jackets mounted on their huge horses surrounded by baying hounds straining to get to the chase. Now here I was in a village where the horses were stabled and the hounds were cared for and trained to hunt.

Over the years I came to understand the relationship between the services that the hunt provided to the local farming community and of the strength of the support that this field sport received from the country people.

The huntsman and the whipper-in are the two employed members of the hunt team. They are under the direct control of the Master of Foxhounds (MFH), by tradition an established landowner in the area who occupies the post for many years before retiring and handing the title to another person of similar standing.

The incumbent MFH, when I arrived at Elham, had only held the post for a couple of years but went on until the 1990s before retiring. The East Kent Hunt had been formed in the early part of the 19th century although its roots can be traced back a lot earlier.

They provided a service to farmers who had suffered fallen stock through whatever cause. The huntsman went to the location and dispatched the sick or injured animal as appropriate. Then he removed the carcass from the land, and it was fed to the hounds. The farmer benefitted by not having expensive veterinary bills, and free disposal of the carcass, whilst the hunt received free fresh meat for the pack.

Police involvement with the hunt frequently occurred following attacks on farm animals by stray dogs. The hunt always tried to maintain a good relationship with the farming community, and the police, to ensure mutual co-operation.

They also had large areas of arable and forest land over which to hunt the vermin which did damage and caused death to stock, particularly lambs and chickens.

I recall being called to speak to a smallholder who kept a few hundred sheep on downland that was owned by a titled landowner.

On several occasions he had gone to the flock in the morning to find injured sheep and lambs, some of which were so severely damaged as to require the services of the huntsman.

The blame was set fairly and squarely on stray dogs from a nearby urban estate.

I had called the huntsman to attend and he had destroyed half-a-dozen young sheep that had injured and bleeding limbs. These were injuries beyond the recovery skills of the vet. The smallholder was distraught at his loss, being of the "old school" he had names for a lot of the individual sheep in his flock. For people like him it was a personal loss as well as a financial one.

Later that evening I was in the village when the huntsman stopped me. He invited me up to the hunt kennels where he wished to show me something interesting that puzzled him.

We went to the kennels and he showed me the fleeced carcasses of the sheep that he had collected from the scene of carnage earlier. He had been preparing them for the hounds' meal and had expected to see specific injuries including dog bites.

Clearly imprinted upon the flesh beneath the now-removed fleeces were round contusion marks some 4 inches in diameter. It then became clear that the circular marks were not complete but were horseshoe-shaped. There were no bite marks in any of the sheep that he had collected. I then recalled that in the same field as the sheep, but well away from the flock, on my visits, were two Shetland ponies.

These ponies were owned by the landowner and ridden by his young daughters, and were grazed in the same field in the belief that the sheep and ponies would co-exist peaceably together.

The following day I went to the smallholding and accompanied the shepherd to his field where I examined the ponies.

Clearly, one of them still had bloodstains around the rear hooves and backs of the legs. It had been systematically kicking the sheep when they came into range, hence the injuries.

I was able to speak with the landowner and convince him that his ponies were responsible for the shepherd's loss and he was kind enough to fully compensate the shepherd and happy to graze the ponies in another paddock.

One satisfied shepherd and even better relationships built.

In the seven years that I served at Elham I was fortunate to have every Christmas Day off duty and was able to spend those days with my family.

There was a good reason for this. On Boxing Day, the Elham Valley Hunt held their meet in the village. That was our Big Day in the calendar.

The event had become huge over the many years that this tradition had gone on. In the 1960s and 1970s coach loads of visitors arrived from the coastal towns where the hotels provided Christmas programmes to include a trip to Elham on Boxing Day morning.

As well as the village folk turning out to meet the hunt, the ingress of tourists meant that upwards of 2,000 people could be expected to join the celebrations.

Our work started as soon as it got light with vanloads of No Waiting cones being set up on the main route through the village. Temporary car parks were set up in the fields and my local Specials were all on duty to assist.

Soon after 10am people would start to fill the old village square to get the best vantage points. The pubs would be open early to serve tea and coffee (?) and the atmosphere would become very seasonable.

At 12 noon the sound of the hunting horn would raise a loud cheer and into the square would canter the MFH and professional hunters, all in their hunting pink, together with some 15 couple of hounds. Hounds were always counted in two's or couples, but I never knew why! Behind the huntsmen came the lady and gentlemen followers on horseback, all looking very trim and smart on their well-groomed mounts.

On a good Boxing Day the riders could number nearly 100. The thirty or so large foxhounds also found the day exciting as they ran amongst the onlookers and were given small treats.

There were always some concerns when people with small dogs were present because the hounds towered above them and this caused some anxiety but I never received any adverse reports. These were country people, by and large, and this was a day for country people to enjoy. The children especially, loved stroking the hounds which were always gentle and friendly.

Their mood only became different when the chase was on. That is what foxhounds do.

The stirrup cup would be passed around the riders and then, after much mingling with the public, the hunt would move off to its first draw.

The large crowds would soon disperse, either back to their cars and coaches or by packing into one or other of the three village public houses.

By this time the police throat was also rather dry and I, and my specials, annually received a welcome sit-down in the kitchen of the King's Arms where festive comestibles had been prepared for us by Dot, the landlady's wife.

I recall that, on one particular Boxing Day, I was tucking into the seasonal goodies that Dot had prepared for us. I had a mince pie in one hand and a glass of Stan's best bitter in the other when I glanced up, past the open door of the kitchen, to see right through to the crowded public bar. Looking straight back at me was my Assistant Chief Constable and the local Chief Superintendent whom I had been totally unaware would be gracing the village with their presence.

"That's torn it. A carpeting in the morning", I exclaimed to my colleague. But not to worry, because a few seconds later, Stan appeared from the main bar and told us that two tall strangers at the bar who had told him that they knew us had left "a couple in the wood" for our later consumption. Cheers, boss!

The general policing of social events was one area that rural police officers had to attend to.

Besides the larger events, like the Boxing Day hunt meet, there were a lot of other occasions where a token police presence was expected to be seen. Many of the regular hunt meets that were scheduled throughout the hunting season were at isolated country pubs where the general gathering of horsey people and the hounds created inevitable temporary traffic interruptions.

The form of these hunt meets had not altered greatly in hundreds of years. The huntsman took the required number of hounds to the venue—usually a rural public house but sometimes a large country estate—where they would be joined by the master and the riders to the hunt. Also at the meet would be the people who followed the hunt across the fields and woodland with the expectation of a "kill" at the conclusion.

For probably a hundred years, depending on the size of the meeting, the rural policeman has been expected to make an appearance to maintain order, control other traffic that might wish to pass by the meeting and to acknowledge the Master.

In return, the Master would ensure that the officer would be "looked after" should he decide to make a visit to the back door of the licensed premises after the meeting had dispersed.

Whilst many people in the twenty-first century would see this type of police activity to be non-productive, I would argue that we maintained a knowledgeable relationship with almost every country person we came into contact with on our patch.

Familiarity was rare, with greetings being exchanged by using the formal address of Mr Brown, Mr Jones, etc., and the constable being referred to by his rank, or by the similar, Mr Kirkbank. By having this regular sort of contact, the police officer was better able to call for mutual aid and assistance when it was needed from the residents whilst they, in a similar way, knew that they could approach any of us on whatever matters that troubled them.

The result was a greater public acceptance of the police, good co-operation, and a generally lower crime rate. In a few words, old-fashioned policing worked in the country.

On one occasion I received a call to attend at the home of a complainant who reported to the office that he had just experienced an assault from a horserider who had been riding along a minor valley road.

I went to the man's home and spoke with him. He appeared very indignant and was showing clear exasperation over what he described as having occurred. I listened to his detail and allowed him to have what is known as a good old rant. By his demeanour and attitude it was apparent that he was the sort of character who was used to having his own way and seemed intolerant of people who did not please him. His route had taken him along a narrow lane, where he had come upon the rider, and was in the process of passing her on a stretch of the lane that I knew well.

My early thoughts were that such an attempt to pass might seem rather optimistic, given the width of road available. It then seemed that the horse had reared up and the rider's riding boot had marked the paintwork of his car. He had stopped and shouted at the rider, a young lady, who had threatened him with her riding crop and sworn "like a trooper". He also volunteered that there had been another car following the rider but he had not taken the driver's name as a witness.

I promised the man that I would investigate the incident and intimated that I had an idea who the lady rider was from the location and description.

I next called upon the address of the horse rider and received the other side of the story from her.

The lady rider explained that she had been taking a newly-acquired young gelding from the field to the stables along the quiet rural lane and was being followed by her friend in her car for the short distance necessary along the roadway, when the complainant forced his way past the accompanying car and sounded his horn before passing the horse and rider.

Basically, he appeared to be rather impatient and not wanting to reduce his speed as he was intent upon continuing his important daily tasks without the inconvenience of horse riders slowing him down. The horse had been spooked and had reared up, causing the lady rider's leg to strike the car because it was too close. Whether the rider's leg was in the stirrups or not we will never know.

The roadway at that point was barely wide enough for two cars to pass. Anger had flared between the driver and rider but it appeared that the driver, perhaps, should have been in less of a hurry, and he had probably displayed a lack of consideration for the female horse rider.

The end result was that I chose rather a lot of careful words to say to both parties, with additional advice, in a rather stronger way, to the car driver to remind him of the greater degree of patience necessary when meeting horses on the public road.

Of course I could have prosecuted him for careless driving and the lady for inconsiderate riding but where would that have led to? I am all for seeking understanding between road-users.

Perhaps in these modern times, with all the pressures on officers to maintain a flow of work to satisfy the monthly figures, such a minor event would lead to formal action and a greater amount of dislike between both sides involved in the argument.

Other events where we usually put in an appearance were at gymkhanas, country shows and the larger alcoholic events such as open air discos and barbeques.

The barbeques sometimes gave problems when gate-crashers found out about the event and chose to spoil the evening by their unwanted presence.

One farmer used to hold an annual event on his land which was a ticket-only event for, at most, a couple of hundred people. It was usual to have a single continuous police presence at the gate, with passing attention given by the local patrol when possible.

The event was held one year on a particular balmy evening, when a full house was expected, so one of our more senior (by age) and thirsty rural officers volunteered to do the gate whilst I, in the 999 car, checked the area several times during the event as a visible back-up in case of problems.

As it turned out, this particular evening was attended by generally well-behaved young people who enjoyed the music, food and entertainment.

Throughout the evening, my colleague—let's call him John—maintained his post at the gateway to the farmyard along with the owner and his helpers.

On each visit I made it was obvious that John's thirst was receiving fairly constant attention, as evidenced by the empty plastic cups on the ground.

My final call of the evening was made soon before I went off duty at midnight and John was still at his post, more or less upright, but insisting that he was still in charge of the gate (he was holding the post tight enough!) and that he would stand down within a short time. Who was I to argue? He would either stand down or fall down. After all, he was with farm people he knew and no problems had occurred, nor were they expected after this late hour.

The next morning John turned up at the rural office at Hythe with a dreadful headache. His recollections of the time between having a final nightcap in the barn with the organisers and waking up that morning were totally gone.

The main problem in his mind was why, when he had got the Velocette motorcycle out of his garage to travel to Hythe, it had not been in the same position as he normally parked it.

I later returned to my village and went to the farm, scene of the previous night's revelry, and spoke to the farmer who was well known to me.

He was initially reluctant to give me an account of the end of the party but, when pushed, explained that John had had a really good time. So much so, in fact, that he had gone to sleep in the barn.

A few of the guests who were still standing decided to take him home, which was about 4 miles distant along quiet rural roads. The only suitable vehicle was a farm tractor and trailer upon which they loaded John. The journey was then undertaken to John's home and his wife was roused and he was put to bed.

His wife had obviously left for work before John woke up later that morning. I received this explanation and then asked, "And his motorcycle got home, how?"

Details of the return of the police-owned Velocette to the rural office garage were eventually forthcoming.

It seems that they could not get the motorcycle up onto the flat bed of the farm trailer so one of the lads volunteered to ride it behind the trailer.

My due investigations into the culprit who had unlawfully driven the police vehicle came to nothing, although I will have to admit to not trying too hard. I was laughing too much.

On speaking to John again later that day I told him what I had discovered and we both had a good laugh at the vision of inebriated farm labourers manoeuvring a tractor and trailer laden with an unconscious police officer, his motorcycle following behind, through the rural lanes, at 2 o'clock in the morning.

It might have been embarrassing if things had gone wrong. Of course, John had still to face his wife that evening . . .

Throughout my time in the village I was to meet many people who had enjoyed interesting lives and who lived in the peace and tranquillity of the Elham valley.

Of course it was the older folk who had the best stories, many referring to wartime experiences, as east Kent was in the front line of the Battle of Britain in 1940.

One of the older female residents, daughter of the local postmaster, lived in the old post office near the square.

She kept a diary throughout 1940 which listed her personal day-to-day activities, as well as mentioning many of the wartime actions affecting the village. These included such events as dog-fights in the skies above the valley, details of captured and rescued airmen and other notable occurrences which she had reason to enter in the pages of her journal.

A researcher and author named Dennis Knight came upon the diary, spoke at length with the good lady and subsequently wrote a book called *"Harvest of Messerschmitts: The Chronicle of a village at War. 1940."* This is a spanking good read as the author has researched the items described by the lady in the diary and detailed the war records of the events from old wartime records and libraries.

There are true records of the numbers of warplanes, both English and German, which were shot down into the fields around Elham, with many of the airmen being rescued or captured as appropriate.

This book lists the diary's events in chronological order with each day's entry followed by Dennis Knight's official interpretation of events—the pilot's details, squadron numbers, aircraft identification and conclusions. It offers great insight into the sort of life endured by the country folk of east Kent during those dark days. There were people like the postmaster's daughter still living in the village and whom I was proud to serve.

Another interesting man was a sergeant in my "specials". I came to learn that he was one of the gunners who had manned "Big Bertha", which was an 18 inch Howitzer gun, mounted on a railway wagon, that ran along the old Elham Valley railway line.

He told me that, at night, the gunners hid the huge gun under the various road bridges that crossed the track. To fire the gun they rolled the wagon into the open, chocked the wheels, loaded the gun and fired in the direction of the French coast some 30 miles away, where they hoped to find an enemy target.

Just how effective such an enterprise was is not fully recorded but the sound of the gun firing must have been a tonic to the local villagers to hear us fighting back.

The effects of the war remained in the village for many years. There was a Messerschmitt dump close to the village where crashed warplanes were taken for inspection, but not removed for several years.

There were bomb and plane-crash craters remaining in the chalk downs and ordnance has been regularly turning up in various stages of decay from the fields and woods since the war.

This ordnance was mostly in the form of ammunition, mortars and small unexploded bombs (UXB's), both explosive and incendiary. Members of the public, on finding these items, usually reported the matter to the police so that the correct action could be followed.

The advice has always been to leave the UXB in situ so that the army bomb disposal unit could safely deal with any threat.

It became obvious that, in the years before I arrived at Elham, the previous advice had not always been complied with.

In 1971 I decided that the area of overgrown weeds and shrubs at the rear of the garage by the side of the police house was in need of clearing out. I borrowed a billhook and rake to tackle the tangled area that had not received attention for a number of years. It wasn't long before I found a metal cylindrical object. Thinking it was a tin can, I raked it out and saw that at one end were fins. Oh dear! I carefully examined the ground further into the weeds and found another—then another.

Next to appear were bombs and other ordnance including grenades and complete large-calibre, live, machine-gun bullets.

Enough, I thought. I contacted the police station at Folkestone to report the finding and then rang the bomb disposal unit in the Medway Towns who came down within the hour.

The officer in charge of the unit advised us all to leave whilst he examined the cache.

The result was a collection of mixed ordnance which was deemed safe enough to transport with great care for due disposal, although some were training mortars from the military grounds nearby and had been inadvertently left behind after manoeuvres.

Many items were, however, still live and were confirmed by the bomb disposal unit as potentially dangerous.

It can be assumed that, over many years, villagers had delivered the items to the previous local officer who probably treated them all as training items and could not be bothered to deal correctly with them. He had merely chucked them behind the garage.

Between Elham and the village of Hawkinge were woodland and fields, then owned by the Ministry of Defence. The area was used for army training, mostly at night, with troops from Shornecliffe Garrison, near Folkestone, undergoing instruction and training for warfare.

In the middle of this army land is a small private estate which was then owned by an elderly landed gentlelady. Her family had owned the estate since the 17th century and she lived alone with her parkland around her. She enjoyed peace and quiet and merely put up with the inconvenience of night manoeuvres when they occurred.

One day I received a telephone call from the lady to say that she wished me to complain, on her behalf, in the strongest possible terms, to the local army commandant because, the night before, troops on a training exercise had trespassed onto her land and had disturbed her nesting birds by firing their weapons and creating a noise.

This was in clear contravention of a long-standing agreement with the MoD that army personnel would not cross her boundary fences which were all clearly maintained and marked on the military maps.

This lady was very much of the Old School and expected people in my position to do the complaining for her.

This was clearly not a job to carry out on the telephone but demanded a personal appearance, by me, at the garrison so I mounted the old Velocette and drove down to Shornecliffe Barracks to seek out a senior officer with whom I could lodge the complaint.

Try as I might, I could not find any high ranking senior officer prepared to meet with me and had to settle for a major who admitted to me that he was aware of the previous night's exercise.

I explained the complaint and he merely pooh-poohed the lady's exasperation. He more or less suggested that if she didn't like living in the middle of a training area she should move away.

It was not my position to argue. I merely reported the complaint to him and he chose to disregard it, stating that training his soldiers was more important than a few birds and one wobbly old lady.

I returned to the lady's home where she invited me in for a glass of port wine, which, for her, was the minimum show of respect for the police uniform. I explained my actions and she listened in silence. I took my leave with a polite apology that I could do no more for her.

Later that same afternoon, I was in the rural office at Hythe police station, sitting with my sergeant discussing local matters, when the telephone rang. He picked it up, listened for a few moments then uttered an oath to the caller, suggesting that he "grow up", and slammed the receiver back on the base. We continued our conversation.

A few moments later the telephone rang again. The sergeant again acknowledged the call with an angry, "Hello!" and listened to the caller. He then stood up from behind his desk, said "sorry" a couple of times, then, with a final acknowledgement of the very one-directional call, replaced the receiver.

He looked distinctly embarrassed and turned to me.

He said, "Did you make an enquiry at Shornecliffe Camp this morning?"

I said that I had and explained the reasons for that mission earlier in the day.

He shook his head and said, "That was Mr Callaghan, the Prime Minister, who just rang from Number 10. He wants you to speak again with the lady and assure her that she will not be having any more trouble with the army and that the major will be advised by his commanding officer shortly."

I still do not know anyone else who has the Prime Minister's telephone number handy as that particular lady did.

Many of my compatriots on the rural section were long in service and had been stationed in their respective villages for many years. They knew their areas intimately. They were reliable and trustworthy, with a demeanour similar to those of the senior constables that I had first encountered at Dartford several years earlier.

One particular incumbent of a village near Hythe was Tom.

He had served in the British Army during the war and, after joining the Kent Police in 1945, had remained in south-east Kent for all of his service.

It was usual, on night shift, to pair up with another rural officer and I was often paired with Tom—a duty which I looked forward to because of his tales from the past and his composed attitude to most emergencies that were encountered.

At three a.m. one fine night we were patrolling along the A20 at Sellindge when we saw smoke drifting across the road ahead.

As we passed through, the smell of the smoke entered the inside of our car, Tom said "Ahhh, woodsmoke!" as if reminiscing about the aroma of burning greenwood, but I thought it was rather too acrid, and said so. Tom replied, "Better just check it out then."

I turned the car round and we sought out the source, which we discovered to be in a small unit of offices set back behind homes fronting the main road. It was clear that an ancient barn, which had been converted into an office, was well alight, so we called on the radio for the fire brigade to attend at once.

We confirmed that the building was secure and there was no indication that anyone was still on the premises. We thought that the best thing to do was to await the attendance of the fire fighters before doing anything too heroic.

A neighbour from the house next door appeared wearing his dressing gown and confirmed that he had also dialled 999 and was there anything he could do.

Tom enquired if he had a long garden hose that we could use to keep the entrance area damp for the firemen to use when they got there.

The man returned in a few moments, unwound a substantial hose and turned on the water pressure which was, I have to say, quite powerful. Tom took the lead in spraying the areas he considered useful, whilst we could see the fire getting stronger inside the building.

A few minutes later the first fire appliance arrived and the firemen busied themselves getting their hoses out. Ahead of them was the fire chief who came to stand alongside us and, frankly, was rather disparaging of Tom's efforts to fight this, by now significant fire, with just a garden hose.

"You can put that stupid garden hose away. The professionals are here now," the fire chief said.

Tom did no more than perceive the comment as a personal affront to his good intentions and turned to face the fire chief.

"When your lads have got their hoses out and water running through them, I will turn mine off. Until then, I consider that what I am doing is helpful," Tom said; all the time pointing the running hose directly at the chief's uniform and soaking it.

"Jumped up little twerp!" Tom uttered. He then turned the flow of water back to the burning building leaving the fire chief cursing and making a rapid retreat to urge his men to hurry up.

After the fire was eventually brought under control the fire officer did spend a moment to come back to us and apologise for his initial remark and thank us for doing all that we could at the outset of the discovery.

Tom did retain a reputation for being blunt, especially when he knew he was correct. He was in the front garden of his police house one morning, pulling a few weeds and generally tidying up when a local retired colonel walked past with his dog.

Like most people in the village, the colonel knew Tom as the local bobby and hailed him with a cheery, "Morning, Clarkson!"

Tom looked up from his work, recognised Colonel Atkins and replied, "Morning, Atkins!"

The colonel stopped abruptly and turned to Tom, "That would be "Colonel Atkins" to you."

Tom replied, "And I am either Constable Clarkson, Pc Clarkson, or Tom, to you, sir."

Colonel Atkins thought for a moment, and then said, "You are quite correct constable. You will kindly bring your wife round to the Hall this afternoon and we can have a drink by way of my apology."

As Tom recounted later, there was no immediate apology at the time of the incident; only the order to attend at the big house with his wife. But he did agree that the colonel was generous with the port wine that day.

Tom's pet hate was being addressed by only his surname, as he considered it the height of rudeness and even brought the local superintendent to notice for doing it.

One area of police work that became second nature to rural police officers was the dealing with sudden death.

The town constabulary could always rely upon the designated coroner's officer to complete the paperwork necessary to satisfy the local coroner but, out in the sticks, we had to do it all ourselves, mainly because the town coroner's officer did not know the area beyond the town limits.

In the country we had three broad classifications of this work; death whilst under medical care in one of the geriatric establishments, death through natural causes at home, and death by un-natural means—suicides and fatal accidents mainly.

Suspicious deaths that could lead to a murder conclusion were, of course, dealt with by CID, and if they were in the rural area the coroner's officer would have to find a roadmap.

I do believe that I held the local record for the least time spent between receiving the report of a sudden death, arranging transportation by a local undertaker for the body to be taken to the mortuary, arranging and attending at the *post mortem* examination, and submitting the blue form to the coroner for his decision as to the cause of death. Two hours, fifteen minutes.

In this particular case I was given the task at 10.00am to deal with the death of a very elderly lady who had passed away during the night at St Mary's Hospital nearby.

She had only recently been admitted to the geriatric ward from her home where she lived alone, and the duty doctor was not in a position to issue a death certificate himself, not being aware of her precise medical record.

I was able to telephone the hospital and arrange for the nursing sister to be present when I arrived at the hospital to do the formal identification (ID). I then telephoned the undertaker who, fortunately, was already on his way to the hospital to deal with another body and I arranged for my subject to go, "double-decked" with his current body, to the mortuary at Canterbury Hospital, after the ID had been carried out. That was OK even though it was not a generally accepted practice.

I was then lucky enough to arrange for the duty pathologist to carry out the *post mortem* at 11.30am, which gave me time to get to Canterbury Hospital, to borrow a typewriter to fill out the blue form in the mortuary, and to have it signed by the pathologist at conclusion of the *pm* at 12 noon. Then straight to the coroner's office in Canterbury for 12.15pm where the Coroner confirmed that he was satisfied that cause of death was natural and wrote out his certificate to close the police involvement.

Rarely do similar cases work out quite so well.

Being a village bobby was a very enjoyable posting, although we did have some quite disagreeable cases to deal with. Whilst not typical of routine rural work, suicides are incidents that have to be dealt with like everything else that may crop up in a day's work.

On reporting for duty one morning I was directed to a house at St Mary's Bay on Romney Marsh, which was at the opposite end of the rural sub-division.

My Velocette carried me down there in 30 minutes and I arrived at a pleasant bungalow facing the sea, where the report was that a death had occurred during the night.

I was met by a gaunt lady who may have been in her 70s. She asked me inside and offered me a cup of tea. I enquired as to the identity and location of the deceased person.

"That's George, my husband. He's in the garage. He killed himself," she said.

My mind then wandered and I considered that it would be a suicide whereby the unfortunate person had probably gassed themselves from the exhaust pipe of the car. This being the most common way when a suicide takes place in a domestic garage. Then I recalled a car being parked on the driveway.

I said, "Have you got two cars, then?"

"No," she replied, "He is just sitting on the motor mower in there by the workbench."

She directed me to the connecting door into the garage. I entered and saw that the man was dressed in his pyjamas and was slumped forward, partly seated on the blade area of the mower, facing away from me.

I also saw a 12 bore shotgun tightened in the vice on the workbench directly in front of him.

I approached the body and saw that the whole of the top of his head had gone and that some nasty looking bits were hanging from the roof of the garage. I made a closer examination of the area and became satisfied that this was a clear case of suicide by shotgun. I then returned to the house with the widow.

Throughout, she remained totally under control, although very quiet. I called for the family doctor and explained the circumstances and he stated that he would be able to attend at once.

I arranged for the attendance of the CID, as a matter of course, and for the undertaker to remove the body when appropriate.

Next, I checked the position of the shotgun and then removed it from the vice. I opened the breach and saw that one cartridge had been discharged and another full cartridge was still in place.

After all, if the first barrel is effective in a suicide attempt, the participant in the exercise would be very unlikely to discharge the second barrel as well.

The doctor arrived and confirmed life extinct, which is a legal prerequisite from a doctor in all such cases—even though it was patently obvious that, without a brain, the deceased was not going to go anywhere.

He also made reassuring remarks to the widow, offering medicaments but they were declined.

The doctor was able to give me details that the man had been suffering from depression caused by severe headaches which, the doctor thought, may have been caused by an aneurism in the brain.

The detective sergeant arrived and I showed him the scene. He turned a strange shade of grey and said he was satisfied that it was a suicide, before having to rush off on another call. That is what he told me anyway. He had no intention whatsoever of hanging around to help the undertakers in their grim job.

The undertaker's assistant took one look at the scene within the garage and immediately rushed off across the road to spend a few minutes leaning over the sea wall.

I then had to assist them in collecting as much as possible of the "matter" into a plastic bag, for later consideration by the pathologist. That then went off to the local hospital, together with the deceased, in the hearse.

I didn't feel very good myself but the person in total control was the widow. She agreed to my offer of getting the local authority cleansing department to come out, if they would, and clean the garage.

I left the scene to make the necessary enquiries about ownership of the shotgun and other related matters.

It was later revealed that the cleansing department turned up the following day and discovered that the lady had already completed the cleaning task in the garage without aid. She really was some tough old bird.

At the *post mortem* I identified the deceased to the pathologist who had been detailed to carry out the examination, and helpfully suggested to him that the medical records indicated the man to have possibly suffered an aneurism of the brain.

The pathologist laughed and suggested that, with no brain left in his cranium, it would be unlikely if such a diagnosis could be confirmed. I then produced the plastic bag containing the matter collected from the interior of the garage and indicated that there may just be an aneurism in the bag.

Once more, the mental stress of dealing with death is countered with a degree of shared humour.

A further cause of death by unnatural means is the fatal road accident and I have to say that I have attended many in my service, none more tragic than a head-on collision on Hythe Hill, between the A20 and the town on the day before Christmas Eve.

Several officers were called to assist as the road was blocked and traffic division had set up a diversion. One of the cars had struck a tree at the side of the road and the young male driver had not suffered at all.

He was very dead upon our arrival. Our job was to have the body certified as dead and removed to the mortuary.

We had to arrange for the removal of the wreckage to a garage preparatory to the traffic examiners carrying out a full mechanical inspection regarding possible defects. We also had to secure any property within the car and ensure that it is conveyed either to the police property store or to the person or persons entitled to receive it.

At this time we did not know the identity of the driver. He had no wallet on his person and we put through a request on the radio to get an owner from the County Hall records at Maidstone. In those days the police could not immediately acquire such details.

When we were able to force open the boot of the car we were horrified to find a large number of wrapped Christmas presents and an army uniform. There was also a jacket containing the man's wallet and it was revealed that he was a serving soldier on Christmas leave, just back from overseas.

He was on a journey from his base to his home at Hythe to make a visit to his wife and children for Christmas. This was a case where any sort of humour was absent and most of us at the scene were rather upset at the circumstances.

My sergeant and I made the distressing decision to, together, call at the soldier's home and give the news to the family . . .

Romney Marsh is the pointy piece of Kent on the border with East Sussex and has a history of smuggling and other mysterious deeds from the past. It is a completely flat area of land that is mostly sheep pasture inland, with housing along the coastal strip.

Up until some 600 years ago it was mostly under the sea and became salt marsh before being drained for agricultural use. It was the southern part of our rural subdivision and rarely caused us too many problems.

Opened in 1927, the Romney, Hythe and Dymchurch Railway is regarded as the smallest public railway in the world. It is a 15inch gauge line with exact scale miniature steam engines pulling miniature carriages along the flat land between Hythe and Dungeness at the promontory; a distance of just over 15 miles.

The train service operates a busy schedule during summer, attracting holiday makers and day trippers. In winter it is mainly closed down, apart from being a school special between Lydd and Hythe during term times.

This line crosses over unmanned, ungated, level-crossings in quiet lanes and we experienced many calls in summer to incidents where cars had collided with trains, although most collisions were relatively minor.

In the 1970s there was a spate of illegal landings of Asian people who had been carried, in small boats, over the Channel from France. The English Channel radar was yet to be as effective as it is with the modern equipment in use today and many illegal immigrants were intercepted after they had landed; either on the beaches or hitching lifts on the main road.

The human smugglers merely dumped their charges onto the gently-sloping beach and sped off again, leaving the poor people to their own fate on a desolate stretch of unwelcoming coastline, miles from any town.

Early one cold March morning Bob, the village bobby at Dymchurch, was doing his early morning perambulations around his small town when he walked across the level-crossing of the miniature railway and glanced over to the normally deserted train station. There was an Asian man, holding a small suitcase, standing at the side of the desolate platform.

Bob put his hands in his pockets and wandered over to the man. "Good morning," he said. "And where are you off to today."

The man replied in very broken English. "I am waiting for the train to London. Can you tell me when it is coming?"

"About six weeks, I think," said Bob, assuming that was when the Easter schedules were to start. Bob gave a heavy sigh and realised that his day was now going to be taken up waiting for the Immigration Department to get into gear.

One winter we had a spate of barn fires on Romney Marsh that were starting to create a serious problem. One huge fire at Ivychurch caused death and extreme suffering to a great many pigs.

After the first two fires it was realised that we had a fire raiser at large on the marsh and urgent action was put into being to try to find the arsonist responsible.

For us, that meant extra night duties listening to sheep bleating in otherwise deserted marshland; not to mention all the inconvenience to our private lives that such duty changes led to.

Late one night the fire brigade informed us that they had another fire report at a farm building near the village of Newchurch, and we dashed to the scene to find a Dutch barn well alight.

As is usual there were quite a few sightseers, even though it was the early hours and the location was miles from anywhere.

Things were beginning to come under control when one of the retained firemen came over to me and volunteered the information that he had attended three of the recent fires. He had noticed that a certain young man, who was standing in a small group of onlookers, had been at a previous fire some 5 miles away and was also believed to have been at the first one as well. He only had the suspicion and couldn't be absolutely sure if it was the same man.

Such information, when given by a fireman, can be very useful but, with no forensic or other good evidence available at that time, an admission was usually the only way to get a conviction.

One of our local police-dog handlers was also present at the scene and I went over to him and told him of the fireman's information.

I asked him if he would be prepared to assist me to have a hard word with the young man. The dog might also help. Paul understood my intent. He agreed, removed his alsation from the dog van and we walked over to where the young man was standing.

"A word, please," I said, and the man somewhat reluctantly agreed to accompany us to a quiet area out of view of others.

We searched the man and found that he had a box of matches in his coat pocket. He did not have any cigarettes and when I asked him to name his usual brand, he could not think of a brand quickly enough.

Paul then told the subject that he now had reason to allow his dog, which he said was specially trained to recognise the scent of arsonists, to sniff him.

He gave a word of command to his alsation, and the dog then moved forward very close to the man and immediately started to bark. That was the standard behaviour of a police dog when told to advance on someone, but it was all very convincing.

The bark was enough to make the young man very nervous and we told him that the dog had recognised an arsonist and he would have to admit his crime or else we would put him in a room on his own with the dog.

By now the man was shaking with fear and sweating profusely. It was then that a full admission was blurted out and noted.

We took him back to Folkestone police station where he made a written statement under caution, including similar deeds committed in Scotland some weeks earlier.

A call to Arbroath led to the offences being confirmed and a good job done. I do believe such an interrogation would not be allowed in modern times but in the early 1970s with little or no forensic evidence available and only scant circumstantial evidence, I think we got our man.

One of the more unusual type of calls we had to deal with were from members of the public who had seen something which they considered was worthy for us to investigate, even though the incident might have been brief, and substantial time had passed before they found a telephone from which to call us. This could be anything from seeing a flying saucer to hearing a woman screaming in deserted countryside. The howl of a vixen on heat is a similar noise. However, what followed on from several sightings of a wild beast by passing motorists on Stone Street did prove to be more enlightening.

Stone Street is the old Roman Road that links Canterbury with Hythe and is, for the most part, a dead straight road passing through both arable and forestry land. Part of the forestry section was within the parish of Stowting and it was from this section of road that most of the reports of "the beast of Stone Street forest" emanated. The beast was variously described as a panther, a lion, a huge cat with a long tail, and even a grey ghost with four legs. It was only sighted at night and, whilst the first reports were treated with a degree of illogicality, the unrelated pieces of information did seem to indicate that there was something unusual being seen in the wooded areas.

Routine checks were made of farms in the area to enquire if there had been any loss of rare or exotic animals but nothing useful was forthcoming. The nearest establishments where wild members of the cat family were kept were at Lympne, some seven miles to the south and near Canterbury, some ten miles to the north. Neither management was prepared to admit any losses of their stock over the past few years.

One Sunday morning, I was given the task to attend at a farm at Stowting where the farmer had reported shooting dead a large cat.

On my arrival at the farm buildings, the farmer identified himself and took me to his Land Rover. He removed a tarpaulin from the body of a very large cat. It looked like a leopard and I recalled the reports of the beast of Stone Street forest.

The farmer related his story to me and said that he had been suffering heavy losses from his flock of sheep and lambs in recent weeks and suspected that he had a fox problem that was getting out of hand. He was a hunt supporter and the local huntsman had been over his land with the terriers but found nothing to indicate any local fox population. The farmer had then, reluctantly, set fox wires into the gaps in hedgerows to try and catch whatever was killing his stock.

Within the first few days, he discovered that some of his fox wires had been removed. It was his regular habit to check the locations at daybreak each day so that if a fox had been caught by the wire noose, he could dispatch it with his shotgun so as to save it from undue suffering. Whatever it was had been strong enough to tear the wire from the branches where the trap had been set. Badgers are strong enough to drag out such traps but they don't attack lambs, and the farmer knew that there were no badger holts on this part of his land, these animals being very territorial.

On this particular Sunday, he had taken his shotgun and walked around his pastures. It was then that he heard a commotion and saw that a large cat was caught by a fox wire and was thrashing about. He immediately attempted to put the cat down by firing first one barrel, then the other, into the body of the cat but his choice of shot was too light and it only served to increase the anger being shown by the animal. The farmer ran back to his house and obtained heavier cartridges, returning in his Land Rover, and was able, with his next shot, to kill the cat cleanly. He removed it from the trap and, after a bit of a struggle, laid it in the back of his vehicle and returned to the farm complex.

Whilst we were discussing what sort of cat it was, the farmer's son appeared with his encyclopaedia open at the page describing a clouded leopard. We compared the dead cat to the description and became satisfied that the son's identification was accurate, given the spotted coat, very long thick tail and huge canine teeth. It was some three times larger than an average tabby cat. Also, the clouded leopard normally lived in the Himalayas. What was it doing in Stowting, in the heart of the Kentish countryside?

After a lot of telephone calls, we established that the only place where there were clouded leopards in east Kent was at a private zoo some considerable distance from where the animal was now. They vehemently denied ever having lost, permanently, any beast of that sort for many years. There was nothing further we could do for the farmer, except to notify the Ministry of Agriculture and a local veterinary surgeon and let them liaise with the farmer for the animal's destruction.

At least the calls to the police station reporting further sightings of the Beast of Stone Street ceased, proving that the previous reports had been credible and not the visions of an imaginative mind.

CHAPTER 19

Time Wasting

DURING MY SERVICE, I have been detailed to be present at three of the periodical visits that are made by a senior officer holding the grand title, HM Inspector of Constabulary. The holder of this office is usually appointed to this high position having previously served as a Chief Constable somewhere in the UK, and his duties include making visits to police forces and "asking the questions which informed citizens would ask" (their words, not mine). He then reports to the government with any recommendations that his office might have for improvements in efficiency, etc. Indeed, an onerous but undoubtedly well-paid little number that, to the bobby on the beat, created a pointless waste of time for everyone involved. The inspections could not be more contrived as they were invariably carried out by appointment, set months in advance.

On the allotted day for any such visit, the cars are polished, the floors are polished, the windows are polished, the uniform buttons are polished and everyone stands around for hours in polish waiting for the entourage to make its appearance.

We, of the Hythe Rural Section, were told that the Chief Inspector of Constabulary and his cohorts would be examining our offices and men at 3pm on what turned out to be a hot summer's day.

Duties had been changed, rest days cancelled, and senior officers were getting in a bit of a panic hoping that all matters under their control would be passed as efficient and professional. Perhaps the telephone should be disconnected for the day. After all, we didn't want any member of the general public inconveniently ringing up demanding attendance at some serious accident or robbery. That would never do.

I had been instructed that I would be the rural beat officer who just "happened" to be in the rural office with our rural sergeant when the entourage arrived, so I arrived early and sat at the opposite side of the sergeant's desk twiddling my thumbs for an hour, waiting.

My sergeant, who was of the "old school" and had made clear his views of this perceived waste of time, advised me to enjoy the experience. He had seen it all before.

At 3.30pm the HMI entered our office with his aide-de-camp. He was also accompanied by our divisional superintendent, duty inspector and, in the passageway, the Chief Constable of our county who had been unable to squeeze into the small office. Introductions were made and the HMI invited the sergeant to describe his duties which were duly outlined.

He then directed several questions to me and I wondered what planet this man was on.

"Do you work nights?"

"Er—Yes, sir."

"How big is the area of the sub-division?"

"150 square miles".

"Do you have a bicycle to cover that area?"

"No. I have a Velocette motorcycle."

"I didn't think they made those anymore."

"They don't, sir. The factory closed in 1968. Mine is about ten years old."

"It still works alright?"

"It is better downhill. Uphill, I have to walk beside it."

"Ha Ha. That's very funny, officer."

"It is not very funny when it is a long hill, sir."

The conversation continued in this vein for a few minutes and I wondered what this man had gleaned from the exchange. I would like to think that the replacement of the Velocettes with Honda 175cc motorcycles some 2 years later was due to my comments—but I very much doubt it.

After the entourage left the tiny office, the Chief Constable entered briefly and said to the two of us, "Thanks, chaps. Sorry he is such an old woman. I've been following him around all day. You only had him for10 minutes." He rolled his eyes up and we realised what a total joke the day had been.

My first experience of an HMI's visit had been very early in my service, at Dartford.

My recollection of that day was similar to the Hythe debacle with several days spent cleaning and polishing ready for the great man, but it had been interrupted by calls to the police station that could not be ignored, and the inspection was somewhat curtailed by working police officers having to go outside and deal with a demanding public.

Dartford police station had been like my first day in the town: so busy that there was nobody in the police station to inspect, so he went home again.

Did he not realise that we were grossly undermanned at Dartford in the 1960s? Probably not.

My last occurrence was whilst I was stationed at Canterbury in the latter half of the 1970s.

A similar format for the visit applied; with little change resulting that would affect policing in the city.

One day, the incumbent will realise what a waste of time such pre-arranged visits are. Either pack it all up, or make surprise visits and actually understand what day-to-day police work really is.

I experienced more time wasting in complying with the system that started in the 1970s known as Staff Appraisal.

This was an idea that was sourced from the business world and was designed to ensure that the right people were in the right posts for their skills and knowledge. It sought to describe the calibre of the person, and to seek out their likelihood of promotion, within a formal report made up of separate reports and opinions from more senior staff.

It was introduced into the Kent Constabulary around 1973 and the excuse was provided that the annual appraisal report would be of prime consideration when officers went forward for promotion through the ranks.

Police Staff Appraisal sought to cover all areas of police work and civil lifestyle and brought together reports from the section sergeant and, usually, two inspectors.

These supervisory officers completed forms for the specific officer under appraisal, and included such subjects as appearance, attitude to the general public, volume and quality of reporting, home life and other areas that were considered pointers to the good workings and attitude of that individual. It should be assumed that all persons submitting this information should be able to truthfully comment critically on these levels.

The whole was then entered into the personal file of the officer, which meant that any senior-ranking officers could subsequently read the information contained within the file and make decisions as to the future of that policeman.

The whole matter came out into the open with the officer's Annual Staff Appraisal conducted by the chief superintendent, usually held around the time of the officer's anniversary of joining.

In September 1973 I travelled down to Folkestone Police Station to have my due appraisal with the divisional chief superintendent and I entered the inner sanctum of his domain.

Whilst I was seated in front of the ridiculously large desk he examined the file in front of him and, after a long pause, described to me how my sergeant had regarded my previous year as having been excellent, and how pleased he was with my involvement within the section. However, both inspectors had described my report work as no better than average and my attitude was that of an officer unwilling to learn from his mistakes.

Overall, a rather disappointing appraisal and one that I should seek to improve considerably in the coming weeks or else there could be action taken.

I wondered whether I should just sit there and say "Yes, Sir," or whether to have a go back. I was incensed that the inspectors had marked me down. What had I done to cause such a bad report?

I decided to argue and said to the chief superintendent, "What mistakes have I not learned from?"

He looked through the file and mentioned two incidents detailed within the paperwork that were obviously recorded as "black marks", but I had no recollection of either.

I persevered and asked for more detail, knowing that they bore no relationship to any action I had carried out. The remarks did not refer to me but to another member of the rural section.

I pointed the error out to him and identified the officer to whom the demeaning report was obviously referring. It was apparent that the report had been compiled on an erroneous identity.

He then mentioned my driving record, with two accidents in the past year. I told him that my driving record was free from any blemish, both privately and in the police. He was speechless because he now saw that the poor reports were unrelated to me.

I asked if staff appraisals had any bearing on future progress in the force, to which he agreed that this was the whole point of having them. I just had to sit back and say "Well. That's my future sorted then."

He agreed to make checks with the inspectors to establish what had happened and, true to form, it transpired that they had me confused with another rural officer whose attention to work had lacked the required effort.

About a month later, I received a written note from the chief superintendent which told me that my personal record had been amended. There was no apology. No explanation and no recall.

The following year my staff appraisal took place in the same office with the same man and I had the temerity to criticise the system.

That did not go down very well and I was later to find out that the particular chief superintendent was on the original group who brought staff appraisals to the Kent Police.

How many man hours went into producing a file that was totally in error, and could well have affected my future service for the next twenty years, I will never know.

On another occasion I had to attend the report of a dead man in a car on top of the hills above Folkestone. The location now overlooks the Channel Tunnel Terminal at Cheriton.

A middle-aged male had decided that he would end his life and drank a bottle of Martini before attaching a vacuum cleaner hose to the exhaust, placing the other end through the quarter light and running the engine, thus filling the car with carbon monoxide gas to complete the intent—which had been wholly successful.

Having taken the job, it is necessary for the reporting officer to remain at the scene until CID has attended, the doctor has certified death, the body is taken to hospital and the car removed. This can take between 1 and 4 hours of sitting around twiddling one's thumbs.

After a while I saw an unmarked police car coming up the hill, and out stepped the chief superintendent who had obviously been told about the death and decided to leave the cosy environment of the town to venture into the sticks.

I got out of the car and expected him to ask me about the situation. He stood facing me and pointedly waited whilst I respectfully put on my flat hat and saluted him. He was obviously waiting for me to greet him officially.

Some senior officers really enjoy the moment. He continued to stare at me and I wondered what he was looking at.

"Who is on the throne?" he enquired.

"Pardon me?" I replied. I had not expected such a question to be uttered. I expected a greeting of some sort or a question regarding my progress in the case of the deceased man in the adjacent car.

I was rather dumbfounded.

"Queen Elizabeth the Second is our monarch now. Why is your hat badge that of the King's Crown?"

I was speechless for a few moments and removed my hat to see what he had obviously commented upon. I then realised that my badge was, indeed, the King's Crown and not the Queen's Crown. The shape of the King's Crown continues up to the cross, whilst the Queen's Crown has an indentation below the cross.

My hat badge had been issued to me by the stores department many years earlier, albeit during the reign of Her Majesty. I hadn't particularly given the shape of my Kent County Constabulary-issued badge very much thought after that.

"It is probably because that is the badge I was issued with," I said, in defence.

"Get it changed, please," he instructed. "How much longer are you going to be at the scene?"

At last. A question about the suicide scene alongside us. "As long as it takes to get things cleared," I suggested.

With that, he was back into his driving seat and away he went, off down the hill, back to the urban comfort of Folkestone. I really do not know whether he was wasting my time or his.

In 1974 I was selected to go on a course at Force Headquarters that would qualify me as an official plan-drawer. Many cases require a scale plan to be prepared and these plans accompany the case papers throughout their journey to the court.

Generally, police officers were bright enough to prepare understandable plans of such incidents as road traffic accidents but such drawings were frequently not accepted in the higher courts and scale plans were necessary. Someone has to do it and I was the chosen one!

Following a week's residential tuition at Maidstone I underwent instruction on triangulation, base line and other methods of scale assessment. Special drawing instruments were allocated to me and I was advised to acquire a full sized drawing board and setsquare, against expenses.

After filling many waste paper baskets with inky hieroglyphics, I finally received written confirmation from the examiner that I could now officially draw plans to scale. This meant that I could be called upon by uniformed or CID officers to measure scenes of crime and submit a scale plan which could be duplicated and used by all parties to the case.

My teaching on the drawing course had been mainly in the metric system, purely because it was becoming more accepted than the old British Imperial measurements and it was easier to work out on a scale. Once a scale plan was finished it could be translated into either metric or imperial, depending upon the measure selected.

My first instruction to produce a scale plan was from the detective inspector at Folkestone who was dealing with a grievous bodily harm offence at a chalet in Dymchurch holiday village.

A plan of the chalet and front path, complete with position of furniture inside the chalet, was required and I set to the task. I took all my measurements using the metric tape measure. On completion I neatly entered the scale as 1:25 and completed my certification.

The inspector called me to his office next day and said that the plan was useless. I enquired why that should be and he said, "I need to know the distance between the front door and the bedroom door in feet and inches. There should be two arrows marked on the plan with the distance shown in the middle."

I explained that, with a scale plan, any distance between two points can be established with a scale ruler. It was not necessary to cover the plan with extraneous measurements. I showed him how to use the scale and when he realised that I was referring to centimetres and metres he threw his hands in the air in dismay.

"But we need it in feet and inches! The magistrates do not know anything about metres. You will have to measure it again in feet and inches," he said.

I tried to tell him that a scale plan was a scale plan, regardless of what units were used, but he cut me short and said, "You will have to go back to the chalet and measure it again. This time, showing feet and inches."

I simply went back to my office and drew in the requisite details in imperial feet and inches, complete with lots of neat arrows, then waited a couple of days for effect.

I returned with the same plan, this time with arrows on it, and he said, "That's better. Sorry you had to go back and use the feet and inches tape measure but we can understand it now."

I then thought that I would be ahead of the game and the next scale plan I drew for the CID was again drawn with an imperial scale shown at the bottom of the sheet but I was later told that they wanted it in metric!

At least the senior officer demanding this modern request realised that only the scale box needed altering.

Chapter 20

In Conclusion

In 1977 I made the decision to quit rural life and return to the town where my two daughters would benefit from being close to school and the other amenities that young people would demand. I considered a move back to traffic division as I felt that my maturity had increased over the years and that I could more readily cope with the work. I applied to headquarters and was visited at my office by a superintendent of traffic division who was to check my suitability for a move. One of the areas that he covered was the amount of arrests and "process" that I had achieved in the past few months. I had to report to him that, as a rural officer, I was judged more upon my overall results in general policing and not by how many people I managed to get to court. His description of being a modern traffic officer was, frankly, depressing as he intimated that numbers of prosecutions was the major area that I should be concentrating on. My views on re-joining traffic division appeared to fade rapidly, whilst he drank my tea and ate my biscuits. The other matter of where I would be posted was also disappointing, as he seemed to suggest a move back to the Medway Towns or Maidstone, both of which were back in west Kent, away from family and friends.

I agreed with the superintendent that traffic would not be a suitable move at this time and after he had left the village in his shiny Rover traffic car I considered where next I could apply.

I got out the old Imperial typewriter and started typing a new application. I decided to go for the city of Canterbury which was only some 10 miles away and well known to my family. The Administration officer had told me that there were police houses available in the city, convenient to schools, and that Canterbury had vacancies in manpower.

With nearly 15 years experience I would be needed for my experience and knowhow. I had discussed my future with my next-door colleague and with other members of the rural section and realised that this was going to be a difficult decision as I had been very contented in my work.

My family remained the major consideration in anything I was to do.

Several days later, with everything finally in place, I decided to pop down to my "local" for a last beer and a chat with the customers.

I entered the King's Arms and was greeted by the landlord who said to me, "Don't worry, Tony. We have got a petition up and it has been signed by everyone who knew about it. There is a good chance that we can stop your transfer."

I was shocked and overcome by this. I had to explain that I had actually asked for the transfer and that I did not mean it as anything against the village. I had taken the decision as being the best for my family.

Stan then told me that they had heard "on the grapevine" that I was being moved out of the village and they certainly did not want to lose me from Elham.

They thought that I had no control over this and decided to act to prevent it happening.

Once I had made my full explanations and bought a round of drinks I was forgiven and offered their best wishes for the future. I returned home and told my wife what had just happened and knew that one of the best periods I had known in the police was coming to a close. I had loved being a rural copper and I do believe that Elham had enjoyed me being their policeman for seven years.

After four years' service at Dartford learning what police work was, followed by three years of traffic policing, and a year in busy Chatham, I had just spent seven great years in a beautiful Kentish village.

It was time to move on to City life and see where the next 15 years of police life would take me.